The PERFUME PROJECT

DIVRINA DHINGRA

The PERFUME PROJECT

Journeys Through Indian Fragrance

WESTLAND NON·FICTION

First published by Westland Non-Fiction, an imprint of Westland Books, a division of Nasadiya Technologies Private Limited, in 2023

No. 269/2B, First Floor, 'Irai Arul', Vimalraj Street, Nethaji Nagar, Alapakkam Main Road, Maduravoyal, Chennai 600095

Westland, the Westland logo, Westland Non-Fiction and the Westland Non-Fiction logo are the trademarks of Nasadiya Technologies Private Limited, or its affiliates.

ISBN: 9789357768337

10 9 8 7 6 5 4 3 2 1

Typeset by SÜRYA, New Delhi

Printed at Parksons Graphics Pvt. Ltd

for my parents, my first scents of home

Contents

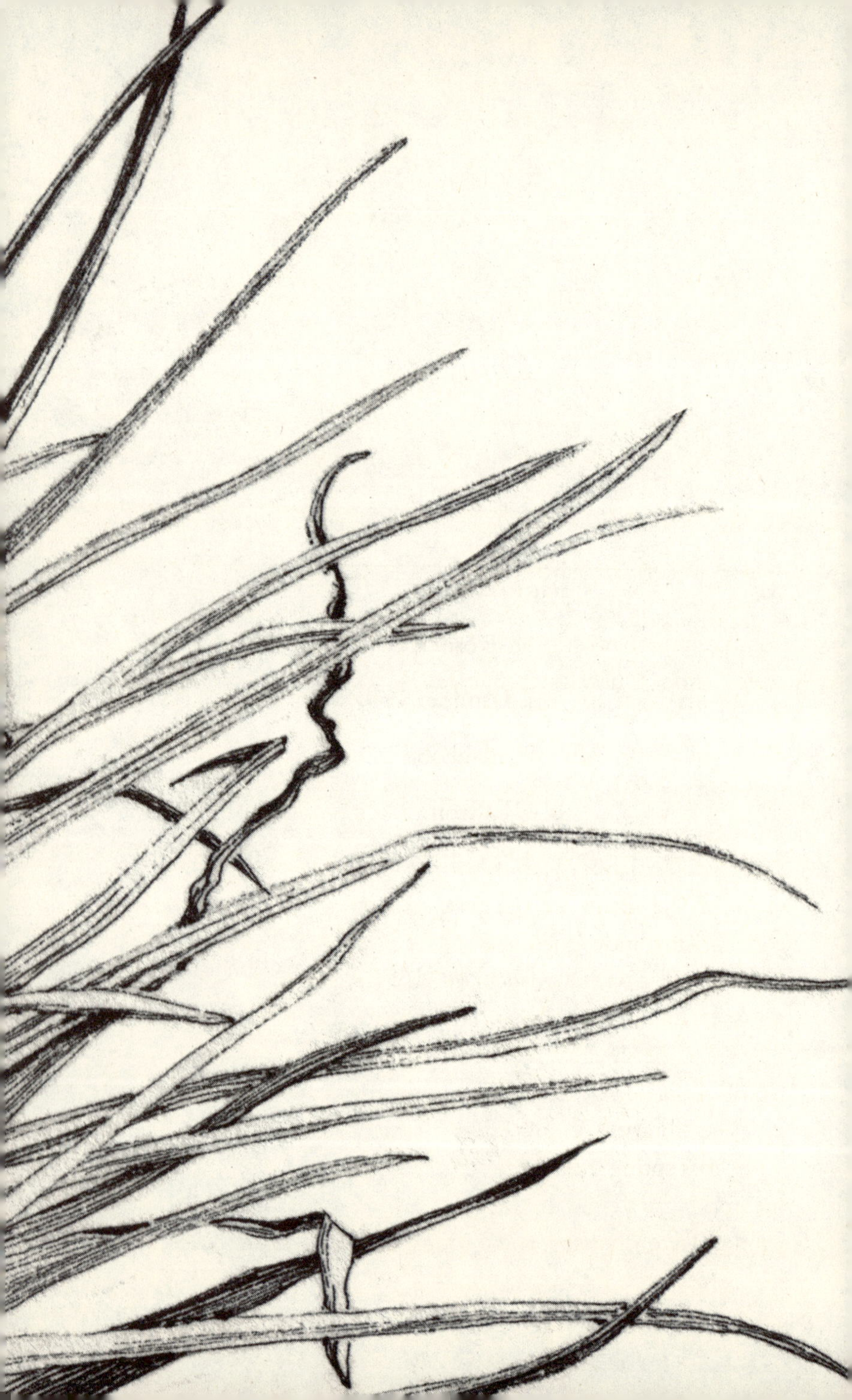

Introduction

I WAS STANDING ON an average-looking Manhattan city block under my university-subsidised studio, outside the coffee shop I usually frequented, staring down my front in dismay. Wilco's *Jesus, Etc.* crooned gently into my ear; there was half a cup of iced soya latte in my hand, the rest had slopped down my shirt and was dripping steadily onto the pavement. I was attempting to minimise the mess by energetically dabbing at it with a bit of tissue when the scent of the scene hit me. Hot asphalt mixed with sweet coffee, rising and mingling with the faint aroma of my own perfume, *En Passant*, with its delicate notes of lilac, rain and, unexpectedly, wheat. They came together to form a perfect fragrance, the smell of New York to me, a beautiful addition to the scent library I carry around in my head.

The library is a collection of memories, catalogued by scent, that spring from a Proustian paraphernalia of childhood memories. As a child, home was a bit of a revolving stage; my parents were divorced and moved cities and states as their jobs required them to, and I moved with them, later visiting these homes on vacation from boarding school. Not quite consciously, I gathered olfactory references gleaned from these homes, visits to extended family, holidays abroad and the spaces and people encountered within them.

For example, the smells of Delhi: the tiny, pale green and unremarkable-looking clusters of flowers on the saptaparni trees that line entire avenues and produce an inexplicably moving scent when they bloom in early winter, the acrid smell of burning leaves, the mysterious perfume of tiny harshringar flowers which bloom in the evening and wither by sunrise, the welcome fragrance of the first rain in June. And the mingling impressions of hot dust, sweet tea, desert coolers and strong incense.

But even when it all became a jumble, when the names of places visited, the people encountered and the important sights started to melt down like a Dali painting, their edges bleeding and blending together, the memories of the scents stayed singularly unmarred. Any one of them encountered unexpectedly could conjure up images of people and places with near-hallucinatory clarity. Conversations that included these fragrant references tended to veer into the unexpected.

'Have you been to the restroom at that doctor's clinic?' I once asked my sister.

'No. Does it smell awful?'

'It smells like Shimla!'

Cold walls, pinewood and hand soap were the smells of Shimla, the setting for several childhood vacations. This doctor's restroom in Delhi boasted of no pinewood and barely any soap, but its location at the back of a converted garage meant that it was dependent entirely on artificial light, which yielded walls that were eternally damp. The smell of cement and whitewash emanated from it, and in that tiny, enclosed space, my mind was able to travel very far through space and time.

There are popular theories that the olfactory is the most evocative of our five senses. Rachel Herz,[1] an expert on the psychology of smell, theorises that the reason for the intimate link between scent and emotion goes beyond the psychological; it is also biological. Both scent and emotion are processed by the same part of the brain—the limbic system, frequently referred to as the 'reptilian brain' (on account of it being common between humans and reptiles), but also known as the 'rhinencephalon', or the 'smell brain'.

Key among the limbic structures, and the one most closely connected to the olfactory sense is the amygdala where all emotion is processed. Unsurprisingly, this is the part which lights up during imaging studies when we smell something. And so the concept of olfactory perception—liking, disliking or being transported by a scent—isn't just innate, but rather more complex. The theory of odour-associative learning developed by psychologist Trygg Engen,[2] an authority on sensory perception, proposes that an odour has no meaning until it is experienced. Only at the moment of experiencing

---

1. Rachel Herz, *The Scent of Desire: Discovering Our Enigmatic Sense of Smell*, HarperCollins, New York, 2007, p. 3.

2. Trygg Engen, *The Perception of Odors*, Academic Press, 1982.

does it take on context, meaning and emotional value. Engen posits that first encounters are especially significant, which explains why so many of our scent associations are formed in childhood. Quite simply, the scents we like were the ones we encountered in a happy or pleasant situation, and vice versa.[3]

And so, fragrances and their associations are deeply and incontestably personal, illogical even. We smell with our minds as much as with our noses, and every scent that moves us can be located within ourselves, as much as out in the wider world.

Through my time in New York, I marvelled at the city's strangeness, the constant hum of self-sufficiency and the scale of it—immense, yet contained on an island. There was the small shock of staving off the cold while looking out of a taxi on a winter night at the valiant, bright lights, and wondering anew at how far I was from home. Manhattan was endlessly engaging, but never very familiar. The city and I never grew to trust one another, and I was slow to realise why.

---

3. Rachel Herz, *The Scent of Desire: Discovering Our Enigmatic Sense of Smell*, HarperCollins, New York, 2007, p. 34–5: 'The odour associative learning theory also has a somewhat satisfying explanation for why it is that of all the world's smells, vanilla is so beloved: Eating has critical motivational value and so does mama herself, signifying love, protection, affection and nourishment. Therefore, when mama is paired with a scent, the scent becomes positive. These early maternal experiences also underlie why vanilla is typically touted as a scent with universal appeal ... it can be explained by the fact that vanilla is a volatile flavour component of human breast milk as well as many milk formulas.'

It had largely to do with smell, or rather, the vacuum left by the lack of it. There were of course the usual ones that bore testimony to lives lived in close quarters: subways that reeked of urine and the stench of garbage abandoned in alleyways, ripening under the hot summer sun. These were tolerated, avoided or ignored. The more intimate smells that signified home, though—dirt shot through with incense, cumin, turmeric, damp soil, the honeyed smell of the night-blooming jasmine growing wild, the acrid one of neem fruit crushed underfoot on pavements—were glaringly absent, replaced by the pervasive non-smell of dazzling modernity.

In the time I could spare from graduate school, I searched for fragrances, sometimes familiar ones in grocery stores, and other unusual ones in perfume stores. I wanted not just the usual scents of sweet flowers and fruits but the ones that had stories to tell, of faraway origins and inspired beginnings. Beauty counters at department stores had a seemingly infinite variety, but deeper exploration of the compositions on those shelves required time and an olfactive stamina that I did not have.

Returning to India, my curiosity regarding fragrance began to turn towards the idea of smell and of home, and how they were entwined. I investigated the tradition of perfume that existed in India, marvelled at its span of history and at how it was, in many ways, the answer to the questions I had about the fragrance of a home. And that is how I started out exploring these perfumes of India, their oils, essences and precious distillates.

~

India is home to some 18,500 varieties[4] of aromatic plants, the volatile oils of which are contained in flowers, leaves, bark, seeds, wood or roots, and have been used for centuries medicinally, cosmetically or both, since, within traditional systems of medicine, the line between categories is a blurred one. The primary use of incense was as an offering to higher powers, but in the earthly realm, it was adopted by wealthy households that could afford them to scent rooms in which guests were entertained, and served as a signage of status. The medieval world in India, as everywhere else, was one where residents were inevitably pressed up close to many more human and animal odours than are regularly encountered now. One must visualise animal-drawn carts and carriages, each adding several pounds of dung a day to the streets, wandering cattle, stray dogs, the odorous whiffs of sewage and decay. Those who could, opted for escape, however brief, via fragrance. As a people, Indians have been concerned with making themselves and their immediate environs smell good for as long back as historical records date.

In the first millennium BCE and for approximately a thousand years thereafter, India was at the height of what is known as the Classical Age[5]—a thriving, vibrant and

---

4. Ramesh Kumar Srivastava, Shakti Vinay Shukla, Sanjeet Singh Dagar, *Cultivation and Uses of Aromatic Plants*, Lucknow, IBDC Press, 2009.

5. Abraham Eraly, *The First Spring: The Golden Age of India*, Penguin Books, India, 2011, p. 3: 'For well over a thousand years, from the middle of the first millennium BCE to around the middle of the first millennium CE, India was an open, prosperous, progressive and vibrantly creative civilization. Indians of that age, particularly the affluent urbanites in the

prosperous civilisation. Towns and cities had mushroomed across the Indo-Gangetic plains, peopled by affluent urbanites who lived cultured lives that included civilised pastimes such as poetry and music, as well as an elaborate toilette.[6] The urbanite, or nagarika, of the time was a sensualist and comparable to a modern-day dandy. He began his day with much ritual in which fragrance played a starring part, taking his cue perhaps from Vatsayayana's *Kamasutra*, which dictates that:[7]

> Now the householder, having got up in the morning and performed his necessary duties, should clean his teeth, apply a limited quantity of ointments and perfumes to his body, put on some ornaments and apply collyrium on his eyelids and below his eyes, colour his lips with alaktaka and look at himself in the glass. Having then eaten betel leaves with other things that give fragrance to the mouth, he should perform his usual business.

Seventh-century Chinese traveller Hsuan Tsang wrote on the subject, 'They are very particular in their personal

---

numerous thriving towns of India, led cultured, fragrant lives characterized by a *joie de vivre* ...'

6. Ibid., p. 395: 'And enjoying every flavour of the city was the nagarika, the sophisticated urbanitea gentleman of means and leisure who had nothing much to do but enjoy life ... Something of a dandy, he spent a good amount of time on his toilette ...'

7. Vatsyayana (Tr. by Shivaram Parashuram Bhide, et. al.), *The Kama Sutra of Vatsyayana*, Project Gutenberg eBook, https://www.gutenberg.org/cache/epub/27827/pg27827-images.html.

cleanliness and allow no remissions in this matter. Every time they perform the functions of nature they wash their bodies and use perfumes of sandalwood or turmeric ...' In the Ramayana, there is mention that Sita was particularly fond of red sandalwood paste, known for its beautiful scent as well as its cooling properties. Later in the epic, Rama's return from an eventful exile was marked by an exuberant welcome by Ayodhya's citizens: its jewellers, lamp-makers, potters, weavers and also its perfume- and incense-makers. Based on these accounts and tales, we can almost see a time when men and women liberally used perfume for their bodies and dresses, with sandalwood paste being a particular favourite.

The toilette of ladies, particularly the well-to-do or those from royal homes, was equally, if not more, elaborate. Indian women of the era would scent their hair, using either fragrant oil or drying it over burning incense, a practice that is also referenced in Kalidas's *Meghduta*.[8] The Sanskrit tale, *Dasha Kumara Charitha*, written by Dandin around seventh century CE, is a collection of stories[9] about the 'escapades of a group of freewheeling young men of noble birth as they go adventuring into the sleazy underside of society in pursuit of wealth and pleasure', and has details woven into the tales

8. Kalidasa (Ed. Kashinath Bapu Pathak), Kalidasa's Meghaduta, or The Cloud Messenger, 1916 edition available at https://avg-sanskrit.org/avgclasses/Books&PDFs/kavya/Meghaduta/Kalidasas%20Meghaduta%20Skt%20Eng%20-%20KB%20Pathak%201916.pdf.

9. Abraham Eraly, *The First Spring: The Golden Age of India*, Penguin, India, 2011, p. 8.

about arcana such as the bathwater of princesses, which was 'mixed with sandalwood, usira and camphor, and kept in gold vessels'. Similarly, Tamilian epic *Silappathikaram* describes the rituals of the courtesan, Madhavi, who 'bathed her luxuriant black tresses, soft as flower petals, in a fragrant oil extracted from thirty-two herbs, mixed with five scents and ten astringents ...'

In his book *The First Spring*, Abraham Eraly often mentions how life in India during the 'Classical Age' is that of prosperous people given to the good life. Far from being frowned upon, such customs, he says, received sanction from the religious belief that the pursuit of kama (pleasure), along with artha (wealth), dharma (duty) and moksha (enlightenment), meant leading a meaningful life. It should thus be of no surprise that Kamadeva, the god of love, from whom the word 'kama' is derived, is said to carry a bow strung with honeybees and darts, each tipped with a different fragrant flower.[10] This aspect of the god has earned him several names: 'From his bow and arrows he is called Kusuma-yudha, "armed with flowers"; Pushpa-dhanus, "whose bow is flowers", and Pushpa-sara, "whose arrows are flowers".'[11]

The importance of fragrant materials that originated in India is a discernible motif in early literature from around the globe, even if the uses they were put to differed. Sandalwood

10. John Dowson M.R.A.S., *A Classical Dictionary of Hindu Mythology and Religion, Geography, History, and Literature*, Routledge & Kegan Paul, London, 1961, p. 146.

11. Ibid., p. 147.

ruled as the most coveted and highly regarded substance. Agarwood was expensive and burning it to scent rooms was a marker of status and taste. Rose water (and later, essential oil) was a Mughal favourite and used variously for fragrance and flavour.

Egypt is another country where perfumery has been in constant, revered use since antiquity. Certainly, there is more, and better documentation, of the tradition there and perfume finds mention in early texts[12] and even tomb inscriptions discovered by archaeologists. Like everywhere in the ancient world, the fragrances relied on plants and resins with the addition of oil or, as in the Egyptian case, animal fat (a variety of animals were considered usable apparently: cats, geese, oxen, even crocodiles) as a base. Scholars have managed to decipher formulae from pyramid texts, the most famous among them being one for Kyphi, a compounded incense that in some descriptions—such as one by Plutarch[13] in *Isis and Osiris*—had sixteen ingredients.[14] But in an inscription

12. Dr Doaa Ragab Fadel, 'History of the Perfume Industry in Greco-Roman Egypt', *International Journal of History and Cultural Studies*, Vol. 6, No. 4, 2020, pp. 26–45. DOI: https://doi.org/ 10.20431/2454-7654.0604003.

13. 'They offer incense to the sun three times daily; Resii at his rising, myrrhe when he is in the mid heaven, and that which they call kyphi about the time of his setting.'

14. Plutarch (Tr. from the Greek by several hands, Corrected and revised by William W. Goodwin), *Plutarch's Morals*, Little, Brown and Company, Cambridge, 1874, available at http://data.perseus.org/citations/urn:cts:greekLit:tlg0007.tlg089.perseus-eng2:52: 'Moreover, that they call

by a seventh-century physician, Paul of Aegina, as well as other Egyptian ones, there are many more than sixteen, and include the Indian spikenard (or jatamansi—a Himalayan herb that yields a woody, herbaceous oil), which would have made it over there via a flourishing trade between the nations when the Red Sea was the principal trading area and its ports a channel for the export of luxury goods from India.

The ancient Greeks—among them a botanist, Theophratus, the first Greek to produce a treatise, *De Odoribus*, given over exclusively to the art of perfumery—attributed the concept of fragrance to divine origin. Though the Greeks were known to make their own fragrances using indigenous flora, they also imported vast quantities, supplied for the most part by the Phoenicians, traders who guarded their routes so closely that, for a long time, the Greeks were unaware of the origins of the beautiful resins, oils and gums they bought. The East was a vague and distantly exotic notion, an idea fuelled by the traders who spun fantastic tales about the origins of their products, keeping demand high.

Among the best-known accounts of ancient Greek trade with the East is the *Periplus Maris Erythraei*, an anonymous

---

Kyphi, is a kind of a Composition made up of Sixteen Ingredients, that is, of *Honey, Wine, Raisins, Cyperus, Resin, Myrrh, Aspalathus, Seseli, Schoenanthus, Bitumen, Deadly Night shade* and *Dock*; to which they add, *the Berries of both the Junipers*, (the one whereof they call the *Greater*, and the other the *Lesser Sort*) as also *Calamus Aromaticus*, and *Cardamoms*. Neither do they put them together slightly, or at a random Rate, but the *Sacred Books* are read to the *Perfumers* all the while they are compounding them.'

work from around the first century CE. Written in the style of a diary, it mentions lands visited, the best commodities available in those countries and gives descriptions of the passage by sea. Its final chapters describe the east coast of India and its ports that received shipments of costus, spikenard, bdellium (a gum used in medicine and incense), cardamom, cloves and sandalwood, among other things.

The Greek love for luxury, perfume included, reached near sybaritic heights, but were possibly short of hedonistic thanks to their belief in the spiritual side of fragrance. Like followers of Islam later, the Greeks also believed that the afterlife was spent in a heaven where every person could find a limitless quantity of their favourite perfume to anoint themselves with—Elysium, for instance, is said to be a land where rivers of perfume flowed, scenting the air above them.

Trade in fragrant substances was a regular feature of Roman life as well, although they were far less interested in the metaphysical side of nature than the Greeks. Theirs was a pure love of luxury and the use of perfumes was far more secular; almost excessive, with practically everything—food, banquets, bathhouses, temples and homes—being scented, despite the official policy of austerity and moderation the Romans maintained when it came to luxurious imports from the East. As with the Greeks, the writings of their geographers, traders and botanists succeeded in exoticising the East as well, a land supposedly populated by giant beasts and barbaric men, which had the effect of increasing the demand for spices, gums, herbs and other raw materials. Pliny the Elder's *Natural History* mentions several races (based, according to him, on Greek precedent) such as the one-legged Sciopods and the Blemmyae, who were headless with their faces embedded in their chests, and were beings purportedly native to regions such as India and Ethiopia.[15]

The Romans dealt chiefly with the Arabs, who did brisk trade with the empire, and had strategic ports such as Palmyra, which specialised in perfumes and became a bit of a manufacturing centre, given the vast amounts of spices that arrived there, much of it overland from India.[16] The Red Sea coast had once been covered in ports bustling with lively commerce, a hub for trade with North Africa, Arabia and India—much more so than the overland Silk Route that gets most of the attention—but these ports have long since been thoroughly reclaimed by the desert. Archaeologists uncovered several of them. The ancient port of Berenike, south of the Suez, revealed evidence that trade between India and Egypt

15. Pliny the Elder, *The Natural History of Pliny*, Project Gutenberg, Vol. 1, https://www.gutenberg.org/files/57493/57493-h/57493-h.htm: 'The Blemmyæ are said to have no heads, their mouths and eyes being seated in their breasts. The Satyris beyond their figure, have nothing in common with the manners of the human race, and the form of the Ægipani is such as is commonly represented in paintings. The Himantopodes are a race of people with feet resembling thongs, upon which they move along by nature with a serpentine, crawling kind of gait. The Pharusii, descended from the ancient Persians, are said to have been the companions of Hercules when on his expedition to the Hesperides. Beyond the above, I have met with nothing relative to Africa worthy of mention.'

16. John Noble Wilford, 'Under Centuries of Sand, A Trading Hub', *The New York Times*, 9 July 2002.

had been more robust than previously known. The coasts of the Red Sea were kept quite busy supplying ships with aromatics, a most valuable cargo, so much so that Indian spices were on the list of commodities that were subject to tax. In fact, Pliny the Elder complained, 'In no year does India drain off less than 50 million sesterces of our Empire's wealth.'

The fabled spice route had a considerable part to play in the medieval Western imagination that had been captivated by spices, the idea of them, their allure and their aroma, all of which embodied the Exotic. Spices soothed and calmed, their fragrance could create an environment that was refined when homes were fumigated with burning aromatic substances, or holy when religious ceremonies made use of them.

Fragrance was directly linked to good health and conferred with healing properties, and perfume thus to symbolised sanctity. Real saints were said to exude a characteristic scent, symbolic of the favour of the heavenly realms, and in death, their corpses emitted a fragrance as well, a sign of virtue. The Bible is rife with examples that correlate perfume with the sacred; for instance, the *Song of Solomon* is thick with the scents of myrrh, frankincense, saffron and nard (jatamansi).[17] In the Old Testament, the Lord commands Moses to build an altar and burn an incense made of spices and resins. The altar itself had to be anointed with a perfumed oil.

17. Paul Freedman, *Out of the East: Spices and the Medieval Imagination*, New Haven: Yale University Press, 2008, p. 77.

Although early Christianity rejected[18] the use of perfume (due in considerable part to the popularity of the practice in ancient Rome) as excessive and vulgar, in the New Testament, for example, Mary Magdalene anointed the feet of Christ with the oil of nard and her offering was accepted. The conflation, within Christianity, of scent with the sacred simultaneously stemmed from and contributed to the assumption that perfumed substances must naturally have their origin in otherworldly places. India, then as a great source and entrepot of perfumes, came, in the medieval Western imagination, to be considered the location of the Garden of Eden.[19]

The centrality of fragrance in daily life and ritual echoed across the world. It made its way into China and further east,

---

18. Writers from the early Christian era, such as Justin Martyr (100–160 CE), argue against its use claimimg that God had no need for such excess. See: Lyman Coleman, *A Church without a Prelate: The Apostolical and Primitive Church. Popular In Its Government and Simple In Its Worship.* Thomas Ward and Co., London, p. 343: 'We who worship the Ruler of the Universe are not athiests. We affirm as we are taught that he has no need of blood, libations, and incense.' Also see: Timothy Carroll, 'The Scents of Heaven', *Aeon*, 24 December 2018, https://aeon.co/essays/frankincense-and-myrrh-were-not-only-holy-but-heretical-too.

19. Paul Freedman, *Out of the East: Spices and the Medieval Imagination*, New Haven: Yale University Press, 2008, p. 88: 'The religious meaning of incense was intense in the medieval period, and the origins of most spices were still mysterious. Spices provided a wonderful flavour and aroma, but their appeal was enhanced by their expense and their origin in a poorly understood geography of the East. Somewhere in the eastern regions of Asia was India, where spices were known to originate ... the Garden of Eden, the terrestrial paradise was known to lie at the eastern extreme of Asia.'

where it arrived with the advent of Buddhism, which, as we know, originated in the Indian subcontinent during the third century CE, where incense was already being used during religious ceremonies.[20]

In India, the consumption of perfumes hit an all-time high during the Mughal period. The emperors and courtiers, aesthetes to the last, elevated the custom to a high art. The first Mughal emperor, Babur, a nomad and warrior, recorded[21] the use of khus grass for building huts and one presumes this practice had the additional benefit of protection against the scorching heat of the Indian summer. His successor, Humayun, having spent fifteen years in exile in Persia, developed a taste for more refined pastimes—especially astronomy—and his court was also treated to poetry, calligraphy, art and, doubtless, the Persian passion for beautiful fragrances.

---

20. Thomas Watters, *On Yuan Chwang's Travels in India 629–645 AD*, London, 1904, available at: https://www.rarebooksocietyofindia.org/book_archive/196174216674_10153425489631675.pdf: Regarding the mythical Anavatapa Lake, Yuan Chwang writes: 'The Buddha and his arhats visited it on several ocassions passing through the air from India to it in the twinkling of an eye or the raising of an arm, and down to the time of Asoka great Buddhist saints came to lodge on its banks. Here was that wonderful incense the burning of which yielded a wide-spreading perfume which released all the world from the consequences of sin.'

21. Anette Susannah Beveridge (Tr. by), *Babur-nama: Memoirs of Babur Zahiru'd-din Muhammad Babur Padshah Ghazi*, Saeed International, New Delhi, 1989, p. 488: 'They need not build houses or set up walls—khas grass (andropogon muricatum) abounds, wood is unlimited, huts are made, and straightaway there is a village or town!'

The *Ain-i-Akbari*, which is the third volume of *The Akbarnama* by Shaykh Abu'l-Fazl, contains detailed information of the great Mughal emperor Akbar's reign in India: his a'in, or mode of governing. Its contents are varied, with descriptions of everything from the royal army and its myriad regulations to those pertaining to the royal store for mattresses. Among them is the chapter 'Khusbu Khana', On Perfumes, which offers a wealth of detail on flowers known for their fragrance, as also information regarding the types of aromas, their preparation and prices during Akbar's time.[22]

These compositions feature ingredient lists that make unsparing use of precious substances of animal origin, like musk and civet, along with large quantities of floral extracts. Not exactly scents for the faint-hearted—by modern standards, these mixtures would be considered practically heady—but insofar as fragrance can be considered a barometer for fashion, they give us a glimpse into Mughal trends and preferences. For example, a composition for 'keeping the skin cool' in the summer appears in the *Ain-i-Akbari*:[23]

> Pound together 1t. best Ambergris; ½ t. ladan; 2t. best musk; 4t. wood of aloes, and 8t. Iksir-i-Sabir; and put it

---

22. Abul Fazal-i-Allami (Tr. by H. Blochman, ed. by D.C. Phillot), *Ain-i-Akbari*, Oriental Books, New Delhi, Reprint 1977, Vol. 1, p. 78: Abu'I-Fazl writes, 'His Majesty is very fond of perfumes and encourages this department from religious motives. The court hall is continually scented with ambergris, aloewood and compositions according to ancient recipes, or mixtures invented by His Majesty.'

23. Ibid., Vol. 1, p. 79.

> into a porcelain vessel, mix it with a ser of the juice of the flower called Gul-i-surkh, and expose it to the sun, till it dries up. Wet it in the evening with rose-water and with the extract of the flower called Bahar, and pound it again on Samaq stone. Let it stand for ten days, mix it with the juice of a flower called Bahar-i-Naranj, and let it dry. During the next twenty days, add occasionally some juice of the black Rayhan (also called black Nazbu).

This composition, containing liberal doses of rose, musk, ambergris, orange flower extract, basil and aloeswood, would likely be an eye-watering, albeit memorable perfume, and in keeping with the Mughal predilection for opulence.

A love of the finer things, as well as a certain streak of showmanship, is possibly what accounts for their unstinting use of precious ingredients. Ambergris, for example, along with its scent—warm, mineral and musky with a touch of marine saltiness—has the additional quality of being perfumery's most prized, most mysterious substance. Surrounded by lore, ambergris (which is French for 'grey amber') has been prized for centuries as a medicine, an aphrodisiac and a perfume. Theories of its origins were several and varied, as is seen also in the *Ain*, where the author muses:

> Some say that Ambar grows at the bottom of the sea, and that it is the food brought up again after eating, by various animals living in the sea. Others say that fishes eat and die from it, and that it is taken from their intestines. According to some, it is the dung of the sea cow, called sara; or the foam of the sea. Others again say that it trickles from the mountains of islands.

Doubtless, this mystery added to its appeal, as did the unpredictability in obtaining it. Most often spotted floating in the Indian Ocean or near the coasts of China, fishermen would often chance upon it by pure luck. In 2013, it was reported that fishermen in Chinnoor village off the southern Indian coast had discovered a large lump of ambergris weighing 15 kilograms in their nets.[24] Some of the fishermen mistook it for jellyfish and were in favour of throwing it back in the water, but one among them, having heard of such a substance from his father and grandfather, saved it and took it to the village sarpanch, who in turn took it to the customs and excise officials. The ambergris was valued at between Rs 15–20 lakh if sold domestically, and Rs 70–75 lakh if sold in the international market.

The *Ain* has a theory that comes close to what we know today about the substance. Ambergris, for all its allure and remarkable worth, is actually the sperm whale's version of spit-up, or a hairball. It comprises the indigestible parts of squid, which forms the diet of the whale, and is later excreted. This material floats along the ocean, and acquires its characteristic grey, pumice-like appearance and scent after months, or years, of being cured in the sun and saltwater.

Two texts from the Indian Deccan too contain extensive lists of plants and substances used in perfumery: the *Itr-e Nauras Shahi*, a treatise on perfumery written in the

---

24. A.V. Ragunathan, 'Fishermen net ambergris in mid-sea', The Hindu, 28 February 2013, https://www.thehindu.com/news/national/tamil-nadu/fishermen-net-ambergris-in-midsea/article4459614.ece.

seventeenth century in Bijapur for Ibrahim Adil Shah, and the *Lakhlakha* written in the nineteenth century in Hyderabad.[25]

The picture of the past thus formed is a bright and busy one. It is one that made the perfumes we recognise—concocted meticulously in laboratories, in scientific spaces of perfect measure and exact formulae—easier to locate in a more accessible world. History provides the link between the clinical settings in which I learnt the precision and concentration required to compose even a simple fragrant accord. Where nature produces the most sublime fragrances with admirable nonchalance, learning to emulate even a fraction of her facility required scales, beakers and pipettes handled with focus. In the lab, in trying to blend together molecules, I leant control and patience with mistake after (often) ill-smelling mistake. I also witnessed chemistry in fascinating action, and the imprecise, messily beautiful universe of people, lands and stories that make up Indian perfume.

---

25. Ali Akbar Husain, *Scent in The Islamic Garden: A Study of Literary Sources in Persiana dn Urdu*, Oxford University Press, Pakistan, 2012, p. 82.

Rose

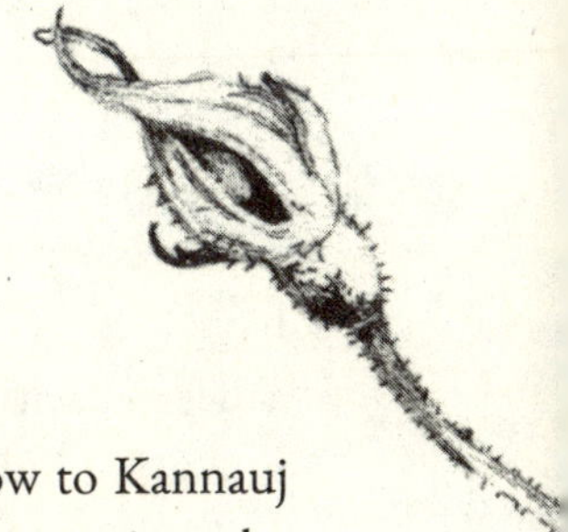

BOUNCING ALONG THE road from Lucknow to Kannauj in Uttar Pradesh, I watched as, in quick succession, the cityscape gave way to the semi-urban and then to the rural, flipbook-like. The construction got lower and sparser, the cars gave way to Enfield Bullet motorcycles with milk cans tethered to each side, and finally, to pony-drawn carts, until I was driving past mud-and-brick huts, charpoys and green fields with scarecrows (sporting turbans and kurtas). I was on my way to see the city that had once been the centre of the region's traditional perfume industry and still held, I hoped, some of the secrets of the craft.

As the famed 'centre of perfumery', Kannauj has acquired a somewhat mythical stature. In conversations about the trade that defines it, the city invariably invites parallels to Grasse, a small town in the south of France where perfumery developed in the nineteenth century as a reaction to the leather industry in order to mask the stench of tanning. Fine leather goods that smelt rank didn't have much of a market, and an entire industry sprang up to produce aromatic plant essences that could mask the odour. Fortunately, the town had a climate (or microclimate) that made growing the necessary plants possible, which is the similarity that invites comparisons to Kannauj. Both towns have historically been hubs for production and trade in aromatics and home to distilleries—

their names slowly becoming bywords for perfume, evoking scents and acquiring a romantic patina. However, though the past was kind to Kannauj, in the present, much of its lustre has faded. Where Grasse has managed to reinvent itself to a degree, with the French flair for preserving tradition via museums, independent perfumeries, tours, fragrance schools and a valuable association with brands such as Chanel and Dior, Kannauj has not adapted similarly to the twenty-first century, clinging still to the old ways which remain a unique selling point for the city—as well as its potential downfall.

The car journey continued, an ceaseless green on either side of the road. The fields were being harvested: women squatting, working with scythes, men manually threshing wheat on rickety tables. I wondered aloud about what crop it was, and received the first (and only) acknowledgement I would get from the driver: a withering look in the rearview mirror and the brief answer, '*Anaaj, gehun aur ganna.*' Grain, wheat and sugarcane.

Lulled to sleep by the sun streaming through the windows of the car and the uniform verdure, I awoke only when we reached our destination. Kannauj announced itself via a small signboard situated on a grassy verge, and with scenes that could have been taken from any north Indian mofussil. I saw it was a village–town hybrid, bursting with narrow buildings simultaneously in use and under construction, traffic clogging it up, the street bordered by hawkers with handcarts and embankments of garbage. A few kilometres later, we finally arrived at the campus of the Fragrance and Flavour Development Centre (FFDC), a government research centre set up in 1991 for the study of indigenous aromatic plants and their fascinating uses. It would be, I hoped, the portal through which I could gain access to the world of Kannauj perfume.

The campus of the FFDC is spread over nearly two dozen acres, most of it occupied by fields of aromatic plants, dotted here and there with squat buildings serving as houses, offices and labs. One such building was the guest house where I deposited my belongings before setting off for a tour with Dr Srivastava, Head of Department for Agro Technology, armed with a PhD and a benign manner. We headed to the herbal garden, a small field with samples of various medicinal and aromatic plants. I noticed rose and jasmine growing there. As we walked on the raised mud ridges that divided the fields, every few yards, Dr Srivastava would swoop down on a plant, come up with a leaf and proffer it to me to smell. I smelt three different varieties of mint (including spearmint, familiar from chewing gum), palmarosa, a green shrub the essential oil of which smells almost exactly like rose, only greener and fresher, and patchouli—famed for its woody, herbaceous scent beloved of hippies—which was an unassuming clump of green leaves growing in the shade.

Dr Srivastava's office was a small room across the corridor from one of the several laboratories in the building, comprising a crowded desk, a few chairs that had seen better days and dust-laden shelves on which lizards darted playfully between yellowed files and small souvenirs and trophies. He offered me a cup of strong, sweet tea and began discussing his thoughts on how the traditional perfume industry was in steep decline, how Kannauj had historically been a wealthy kingdom, and that even a decade prior, perfume had contributed to its relative prosperity through 400 active distilleries. That number had dwindled over time to a mere half dozen. I questioned him on how popular itr was at present, with most people never having actually smelt it, and he confirmed that while itr had once been considered a greatly coveted luxury, its public perception had diminished. With my interest in these ancient and potent perfumes, it appeared that I was an anomaly in these times of mass-manufactured, department-store fragrances.

'But isn't itr very strong?' I asked, attempting to excuse the modern perfume wearer. 'Nowadays, no one seems to have a taste for perfumes like that.' I stopped short of adding 'not even me' to that sentence, but it is a fact that, to an unaccustomed nose, itr can seem far too potent, its opulence too conspicuous.

'Well, itr has no top note, so only the person wearing it can really smell it,' he said.

He was right, of course. When we sample a perfume, we are trained to spray it on our wrists, and that is how we judge it. One does that with itr too, rolling it on or dabbing it from its vial, and as you bring your nose close to it, the smell you receive is rich and almost solid. The ingredients determine the perfume of course, and while a few can be brash and pungent, a well-made itr is surprisingly luminous. As a blend of pure, undiluted essences, it demands a certain respect and a constraint with application.

Any perfume consists of three parts: a top, heart and

base note, classified according to their relative volatility, or if looked at inversely, according to their relative tenacity with regard to skin. The top notes, most often citrus and green notes, are what float off first, diffusing fastest into the air around them, fulfilling their purpose of drawing the curious nose in, seducing it to explore further. Middle or heart notes are usually florals, sometimes spices. These give a perfume body and warmth, and close the wide gap between the light top notes and the rich base notes. Quite literally, they put the heart into a fragrance. The base note is the scent that lingers longest on the wearer's skin, the most intimate, and the note still perceivable after all the others have evaporated—musk, civet, sandalwood, benzoin and vetiver to name a few. But outlasting other notes is not all it does; a good base note also allows other elements to prevail longer, anchoring them, acting as a fixative. This procession of notes follows a set 'physical law'.[26] But what really loosens the molecules and agitates them enough to lift off is the heat of your skin, making it an excellent testing ground for a fragrance.

In the days of yore, it appears Indian itr exclusively used a base note of sandalwood. Foremost among the category of woody notes, sandalwood reigned supreme. In any itr, after the voluptuous floral note of rose, jasmine or a spice has had its say, the wearer is left with a deliciously creamy, soft and warm note that stays on, close to the skin. And, as Dr Srivastava pointed out, there is no top note that floats out

26. Luca Turin, *The Secret of Scent: Adventures in Perfume and the Science of Smell*, Ecco, New York, 2006, p. 37.

and tempts you, departing soon after its job is done. The composition of an itr may be simple, a single ingredient or two at most, but its beauty lies in that simplicity. Even if unfamiliar, even if unpleasant to a nose used to other things, an itr, like the natural ingredients it is made of, is incontestably layered and rich. For this reason, these traditional perfumes demand something of the wearer. A commitment, a little patience, as the perfume communes with skin and reveals itself.

Unfortunately, pure sandalwood oil is now prohibitively expensive, worth more than gold, and far harder to access. Traditionally, Mysore sandalwood has been an integral part of a good itr, but the story of that precious Indian wood is laced with tragedy, and it was a tale I knew I would need to follow to really understand this craft of traditional perfumery and the challenges before it.

The following morning, after a breakfast of more saccharine tea and paranthas at the FFDC dining hall, I set out for a nearby field that harboured a few popular varieties of flowers, including roses. With the windows of the Ambassador rolled down, it was easy to follow the trail there. It was precisely that fragrance of early morning sunshine and damp soil overlaid by the magical scent of fresh roses that I imagine perfumers spend their lives trying to bottle. The aroma of a freshly dew-covered rose is a chimaera though, and I have not yet come across a perfume that managed to replicate its delicacy.

My memories of rose-based fragrances hark back to a childhood spent inhaling my mother's preferred perfume,

Yves Saint Laurent's (YSL) iconic *Paris*—a neon burst of roses, violets and sweet vanilla, tempered somewhat by the scent of her starched sari. *Paris* was neither subtle nor delicate. It was an unabashedly glamorous perfume. That sweet, rose-drenched scent, however, came to represent much more to me than mere glamour.

I took deep breaths of the delicious air once we disembarked and began walking across the farm, rose bushes rising on either side, to meet their owner. The land belonged to Gopal Saini, fifty-seven years old, a third-generation horticulturist. He had been doing this since he was ten. 'My father worked here,' he told me. 'I would travel here every day from our home in the city, four kilometres away, with his food and then helped him pick the flowers—the same flowers I grow now—genda, bela, gulab.' Marigold, jasmine, rose. The roses were next to the bushes of fragrant white bela flowers and the sunny yellow and orange plots of marigolds grown for decorative purposes, not for use in perfume. There were also a few bushes of juhi flowers, the tiniest of the jasmine family with a fragrance less heady than that of the bela flowers—a quieter, prettier version.

The rose used for ruh and itr is the *Rosa damascena*, but Saini grows a different variety: the *Rosa chinensis*, locally known as 'chinia gulab'. Less fragrant and with a low oil percentage, the chinia gulab grows throughout the year and has a less erratic yield than the more high-maintenance damascene variety. There was something poetic about this. The steady, dependable Chinese flower, able to boost a livelihood despite the odds, and the romantic damascena, too demanding to be sustainable. The local variety was put to use for what are now Kannauj's flagship rose-based products: rosewater and gulkand, the latter a sort of compote made by layering sugar and rose petals and letting them mature, an effective and beautifully scented digestive aid.

Kannauj, not so long ago a rich kingdom famous for its rose-based itrs, no longer grew the oil-rich flowers required for rose itr. Those grew elsewhere in Uttar Pradesh, where the conditions were more favourable, and I planned on visiting them to understand the difference myself.

Later that day, I visited the factory premises of Pragati Aroma, one of the larger perfume distilleries. Pushpraj Jain (whose first name, when translated, means the 'ruler of flowers', a possible reference to Lord Brahma) was a second-generation perfume-maker and a pillar of society, doing charitable work such as funding a free ambulance service in Kannauj. A man of prosperous girth, he wore his crisp, cream-coloured shirt loose over his trousers. We sat in his visitors' room across a smoked-glass coffee table; on the far wall, a large LCD television carried on with a promotional film for Pragati Aroma. In my faded salwaar kameez without a dupatta, with bulbous grey-and-blue sneakers on my feet, all chosen with the morning's field visit in mind, I felt like someone who had misinterpreted the dress code at a party entirely. He was pressing upon me a plate of tricoloured mithai covered in bits of delicate silver flakes.

'These are made at my home, they are very good for you, very healthy,' said Jain, nudging the plate forward. 'And they have a bit of our own pure rose oil. After you eat one, when you burp, you'll taste roses for the rest of the day!'

A luxury indeed. Pure rose oil is a prized material, labourious to produce and, consequently, extremely expensive, clearing over Rs 10 lakh per kilogram. Putting the pure oil of rose to work to flavour food was a practice I assumed had died out with the Mughal court.

But then, in Kannauj, it looked like the past never went anywhere. On the drive to the factory through the narrow lanes of the historic city, I gazed at the cracked streets that didn't seem to belong to the present as we know it. These lanes had once been part of a seventh-century fort that was built during the reign of the Pushyabhuti king, Harshavardhana, but now, with the fort and the king gone, only the lanes remained—narrow and twisting in some places, steeply uphill in others, flat at times. On either side were dwellings of mud brick with tiny doors painted in bright colours. The Ambassador trundled slowly, jostling for space with buffaloes being placidly herded along, stopping occasionally to drink from stone troughs built along the side of the road for that purpose.

In such stately manner did I arrive at Pragati, which announced itself by the scent of spicy itr hanging heavy in the air. This distillery employed the traditional technique that is still widely used in Kannauj. It was an ancient set-up for the most basic kind of distillation, consisting of a deg, a round kettle and a receiver, or condenser, called a bhapka. The two were connected by a bamboo pipe, through which steam

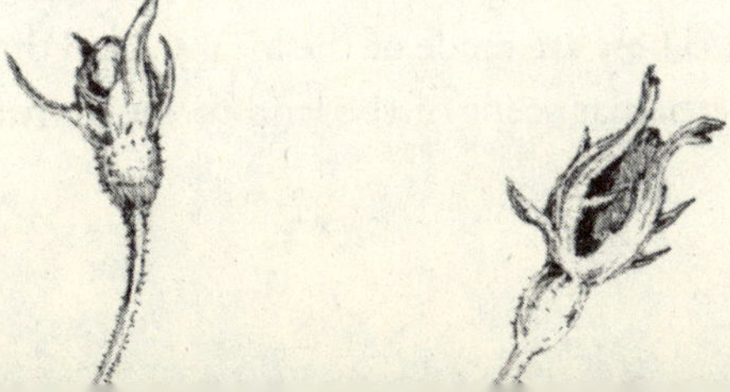

from the kettle containing the flower and water mixture reached the copper receiver containing the sandalwood oil or equivalent base material, and was sat in a small bath to keep it cool and aid condensation. The bamboo pipe, or chonga, was wound with coconut coir to absorb heat.

It was the time between harvests—too early in the winter for vetiver, too late in the year for flowers. The only perfumes in production were the spice- and wood-based ones, namely itr hina and mitti itr, arguably the town's most famous export. Much has been written about how well it captures the smell of fresh rain on dry soil, and with good reason.

I had first encountered mitti itr while on an excursion to seek out traditional perfumes in Delhi. After a few false starts, I washed up at the venerable Gulabsingh Johrimal store in Old Delhi, a family-owned retail business, where I discovered this sublime scent among the samples—the bottled essence of a summer monsoon. Its purpose, like with most traditional Indian perfumes, is loftier than mere loveliness; it is used during the height of the scorching north Indian summer to soothe the overheated mind and reassure it of the coming relief of the rain. A few drops on a handkerchief delicately applied to the nostrils is enough.

Its formula, as is the case with most itrs, is minimal, but the unique making practice of it is so much a part of the Kannauj that has survived time unchanged. The finest mitti itr is made not just from any old baked earth, but from kulhars, the terracotta tea cups used at small tea stalls everywhere—or at least wherever they have not yet been supplanted by plastic or styrofoam. These are made of the local soil, all the better to impart the particular scent of the land to the perfume. From an aromatically chemical point of view, this particular smell can be attributed to geosmin, a molecule in the compound produced by the soil-dwelling bacteria that secrete it into the ground. From there, it is distributed by rain, spread into the air and then detected by human noses.[27]

The kulhars formed a small hillock, lit by shards of autumn sunlight. They are to be distilled over a base (almost always a neutral chemical solvent that replaces sandalwood oil). The process is repeated several times over in order for the two substances to really mingle and produce an itr of sufficient potency, which can take as long as a fortnight. Judging when it is ready is the forte of the practised nose, here the kaarigar, a grizzled old man in a dhoti who also kept the fires stoked, and who had no answer to my question of 'How?' beyond a shrug and the cryptic '*Hume pata lag jaata hai* (I can always tell)' that gives away nothing but the reality of how undervalued his job is. Creating this or any itr here in Kannauj is a craft and the men skilled in it are irreplaceable. The ways they have developed of knowing—the perfect temperature, when a bhapka is full, when a fragrance is ready—are skills acquired by time and patience alone.

I peered into the hut where the rows of simple distillation units were lined up on a rough mud floor. The picture—shafts of sepia-tinted afternoon light, frail from the onset of winter, pouring in through gaps in the tin roof past the hazy

27. 'It's been estimated humans can detect geosmin at concentrations as low as 5 parts per trillion, which is roughly equivalent to a teaspoon of geosmin in 200 Olympic swimming pools.' Compoundchem.com: The Chemical Components Behind the Smell of Rain.

plumes of woodsmoke curling out from the fires beneath the degs in use—captured a sliver of existence from a mellower age, one that had somehow persisted into the harsher modern world.

In a storage room a little away from the distillery lay another treasure: two big bowls of a dark, velvet-green itr shamama, a spicy, more complex perfume; a mix of hydrodistilled mehendi flowers blended with a long list of ingredients, mostly spices, but the exact composition of which no itr-maker will reveal. Each maker's shamama is distinct. Some are muskier or spicer, others earthier or more resinous, still others more heavily floral. This particular one was spicy, with a smoky note. I inquired of the workers in the room what substance gave the itr that characteristic note, but got only vague replies. One worker said it was extracted from the scales of a particular fish, another insisted it was made from a particular shell.

A mystery ingredient.

It is a story tailor-made for the Western imagination, fired in great part by lore and imagery that accumulated in the wake of Alexander's travels[28] and conquest of parts of India.

28. Paul Freedman, *Out of the East: Spices and the Medieval Imagination*, Yale University Press, New Haven, 2008, p. 92–3: 'According to one popular tale that began with a Hebrew account in the twelfth century, Alexander the Great decided to look for paradise once his army reached the banks of the Ganges. Alexander and his companions found themselves sailing along the walls of an immense fortified city that seemed to have no entrance. After three days they came to a window and a man appeared there informing them that this was the abode of the blessed, and they might not

Stories of wealth and the strange and fantastic abounded. India was home to many marvels, and where these existed, so too did fragrant spices and other treasures that came from the East. What part had this air of enigma played in the craft of traditional perfume-making in India? How much did it still?

As we spoke, Jain signalled to a worker, who left the room and returned bearing two tester strips dipped in oil. One of these was handed to me with a flourish and an expectant air. I dutifully sniffed it, but my nose, fatigued after having been put through its paces, inhaling sandalwood, mitti itr, shamama and hina, couldn't discern anything more than that the smell was floral and overwhelming. I gave up and asked what it was. It was pure rose essential oil, I was told, disapproval at my failure to instantly recognise it ringing loud.

Although every perfumer acknowledges the superiority of nature, the roses that we are used to smelling in colognes owe more to human ingenuity, which, to create an aroma more real to our noses than any extract, relies on a variety of synthetic molecules—like phenylethyl alcohol, geraniol, rose oxide, citral or damascones—cleverly mixed to produce a scent as fresh, fruity or sweet as you'd like.

'That strip you are holding has been dipped in oil that costs several lakhs a kilo!' Jain huffed. I smiled sheepishly,

---

enter. He gave Alexander a stone to take back with him that was heavier when weighed than any amount of gold, but that once sprinkled with dust became extremely light. It was symbol of glory and fame in the face of death, and Alexander understood its humbling message.'

clearly the correct response because then he offered me the chance to see something I had been wanting to since I began this journey: the rose harvest. It takes place in spring, in Etah, and also in Uttar Pradesh, the source of almost all of India's damascena roses. I had every intention of taking up his invitation.

Over a final cup of tea, Jain revealed that he had found it necessary to diversify in order to keep the business alive. Unlike others who added on unrelated businesses like cold storage for potatoes or dealerships for scooters, he had expanded Pragati Aroma to include modern, alcohol-based perfumes with a factory in Maharashtra.

'The younger generation are liking only deodorants, so we must move with the times,' he sighed, scratching his chin. I pressed him for further information about the secret ingredient behind that smoky note in the itr shamama at Pragati Aroma. It turns out that comes from the extract of seashells, or nakh, possibly the closest material in modern perfumery to the Red Sea molluscs[29] that were used in ancient Egyptian perfume formulas. To get a better look at this unusual raw material, I was directed by the FFDC to the factory premises of Munnalal & Sons. And so, I found myself in another tin-roofed distillery where, through clouds of smoke, I could see a smaller, more crudely made variation

---

29. Alfredo Carannante, Marek Adam Woźniak, Iwona Zych, 'More than just food from the sea: Exploitation of marine resources in Hellenistic Berenike on the Red Sea (Egypt)', Journal of Archaeological Science: Reports, Vol. 44, 2022, 103515, ISSN 2352-409X.

of the deg and bhapka units, emitting a smell that was like petrol, ammonia and leather. Om Prakash Pathak, managing director of the factory, advised caution in sniffing his product. The smell had been known to cause people to black out for a few minutes if they got a noseful of it. I backed away a few steps.

I had arrived too late to see the raw material; it had all been put into the distillation unit, but the tang of its distillate was ferocious. 'This is called choya nakh,' Pathak said. 'Choya' referred to the process by which the extract was obtained, namely dry distillation, in which the raw material is heated without the use of a carrier such as alcohol or water, which results in producing the distincty phenolic, leathery aspect. The round clay vessel being used was an almost exact replica of a distillation apparatus unearthed at Taxila,[30] now housed in an archaeological museum in Pakistan. It dates back to approximately 3000 BCE, which places it several thousand years earlier than most sources date the invention of distillation. The nakh-roasted shells are dry distilled over benzoin. The drops of oil that condense in the long, goose neck of the apparatus are later collected—a long, labourious process with limited yields.

Pathak's family has been in the business for over a century, producing traditional perfumes at this very site. There was a homely feel to the premises. The family's buffaloes were

30. Pranab K. Chattopadhayay, Satyakam Sen, 'Taxila Mirrors Preserved in India and Technology Transfers', *Indian Journal of History of Science*, 54.2 (2019) 135–43.

around, as was a folorn old haveli, now abandoned, built by his grandfather after whom the factory was named. The industry had been going strong in Pathak's grandfather's time, and proof of that existed in Banaras, where Pathak said a particular type of paan has been named after his grandfather: the Munnalal paan, perfumed with a bit of khus in the hot summer, and with hina in the cold months. As he related all this, Pathak's voice took on an edge. Those were the days when the itr trade and craft still drew respect. But now, he told me flatly, 'The itr business is dying.'

The scarcity of sandalwood had led him and other manufacturers to adopt synthetic bases, such as dioctyl phthalate. There was also a decrease in the market share. The fashion had receded, and industries that had been big users of itr—like incense and soap—now preferred cheaper alternatives. The only major buyer left was the chewing tobacco industry, since zarda and gutka were flavoured with natural essences. The case for both those products being banned was in the courts, and all of Kannauj was awaiting the verdict anxiously. In the meantime, Pathak's only other buyers were a few large temples in Rajasthan and Madhya Pradesh that used itr as a part of the daily ritual offerings to deities.

As I drove away from the factory premises, I mused over something that I'd read. In *The Secret of Scent*, biophysicist Luca Turin had put forth the idea that perfume was not so much about either memory or sex as advertising campaigns would have you believe but about intelligence and beauty, in the way that all art is. In the case of traditional Indian perfume, it was also about history, tradition (if a disintegrating one) and perhaps, most importantly, determination to carry on the said crumbling tradition.

February was at a close; the persistent, soupy fog that had become a fixture of life in Delhi had finally lifted. The sun was out in between occasional showers and, all along the central avenues, beds of petunias and daisies were in riotous bloom. Spring had arrived, and with it, I hoped, the chance to remind Jain of his invitation to visit his rose fields and see the annual harvest. I fished out his visiting card from the pages of my notebook which, even four months later, smelt lingeringly of rose oil. The phone conversation was brief. After reintroducing myself and gently jogging his memory, I got to the point.

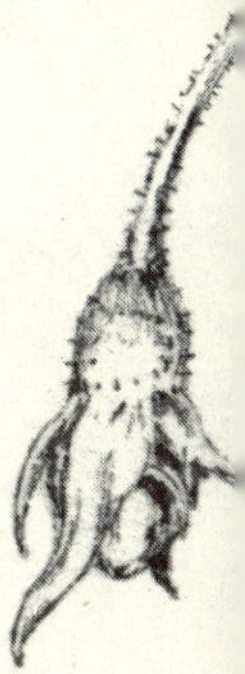

Could he let me know when the harvest was likely, so that I could make my travel arrangements? Sadly, no, he could not, because there was no definite date as yet. The unseasonal rain, a moderate inconvenience in the city, had played havoc on all crops. The rose harvest was delayed by a few weeks at the very least. If I wanted to plan my visit more exactly, I should call not him but his brother, Atul Jain, one of four brothers who manned the business and the one best placed to assist me. He gave me a number and wished me luck with my research.

A famously sensitive bloom, the rose requires the climate to be within precise parameters if it is to fulfil its fragrant potential. Despite its demanding nature, the cult of the rose is widespread, its associations with love and beauty universal. Though it finds fleeting mention in a few Sanskrit texts, credit for the cultivation of roses and their use as ornament and perfume goes to the Persians who historically had a passion for the flower. It is not surprising then that credit for the flower's Hindi name, gulab, come from 'gul', the Farsi word for flower, and 'ab' for water.

The Persian province of Fars: home to the Sassanian rulers (200–635 CE), about whom the only descriptions available are those of later Arab geographers, mainly travel guides written in the ninth century for the benefit of devout Muslims making the pilgrimage to Mecca. These books speak of Sassanid palaces, their beautiful gardens and natural springs. Their stories mention the legend of a particular lake in Firuzabad, said to have been created by Alexander. Later drained by the Sassanian king Ardashir I, it was renowned for the beautiful roses that sprang up on the lake bed. Hence, the 'gulab'. The rose water distilled here was exported to Egypt, China and India, and the region of Fars, home to several valleys, did brisk trade in various perfumes distilled from local aromatic plants such as jasmine, oranges, lily and narcissus.

The first Mughal emperor, Zahiruddin Muhammed Babur, was also the first of the great Mughal naturalists. When he reached Agra in April 1526 after winning the decisive battle against the Sultan of Delhi at Panipat, he was nearly half-dead from the unexpected heat of the plains and facing a possible mutiny from his own soldiers who yearned for home. Recognising their longing as his own, he persevered and laid down the bagh-i-gul-afsha (later the site of the Ram Bagh) in the char bagh style natural to the land of his birth, Ferghana. Terraces, waterways, fruit trees and fragrant flowers featured prominently in the gardens. It has been recorded by the emperor in his memoirs[31] that he had planted 'in every border, rose and narcissus in perfect arrangement'. In fact, the Islamic notion of paradise as a walled garden also finds its origins in the old Iranian 'paridaeza', referring to a walled garden. The concept travelled with the Mughal emperors to India, where, though gardens existed and nature was revered, the concept of imposing symmetry on them was an alien one.

Mughal Indian history, as recorded by travellers and foreign ambassadors to India, is littered with references to the nobles' prodigious use of rosewater and rose oil,[32] among several other perfumes. Rose was used to scent rooms and clothing, flavour food and, in one memorable mention, perfume the horses of nobleman,[33] as a show of his wealth

31. Anette Susannah Beveridge (Tr. by), *Babur-nama: Memoirs of Babur Zahiru'd-din Muhammad Babur Padshah Ghazi*, Saeed International, New Delhi, 1989: '... then in that charmless and disorderly Hind, plots of garden were seen laid out with order and symmetry, with suitable borders and parterres in every corner, and in every border rose and narcissus in perfect arrangement.'

32. Abraham Eraly, *The Mughal World: Life In India's Last Golden Age*, Penguin Books, India, 2007, p. 95: 'Upper class men were heavily perfumed. "All persons in India being extremely choice about, and fond of, scents and flowers, they disburse a great deal for essences of many kinds, for rosewater, and for scented oils distilled from different flowers," says Manucci.'

33. Ibid., p. 95: 'Sometimes even their horses were perfumed. "Everybody in India knows how dear and scarce essence of roses is ... Yet neither scarcity nor high cost deterred this general (Jafar Khan) from having his horses rubbed with this liquid as a matter of course," reports Manucci.'

and his love of fragrance. Indeed, rose oil was discovered in India during the reign of Jahangir, Babur's great-grandson, by the empress Nur Jahan's mother.[34] When distilled, the oil was found to be far more effective as a perfume than rosewater, and was thereafter christened *Itr-i-Jahangiri*, in honour of the Emperor.

~

It was the first of April when I finally set out from Delhi to Aligarh to get a glimpse of the annual gathering of the roses, an ancient tradition in the part of Uttar Pradesh which is the Doab—the land between the two rivers, Ganga and Yamuna—and extremely fertile. I was to go to Aligarh, stay the night and carry on the following morning to Etah, where I would meet Atul Jain (who, I had the distinct feeling, was beginning to lose his patience with me and my persistence).

---

34. Alexander Rogers (Tr. by), *Tuzuk-i-Jahangiri: Memoirs of Jahangir*, available at: http://www.archive.org/details/tuzukijahangirio00jahauoft: '... this itr is a discovery which was made during my reign through the efforts of the mother of Nur-Jahan Begam. When she was making rose-water a scum formed on the surface of the dishes into which the hot rose-water was poured from the jugs. She collected this scum little by little; when much rose-water was obtained, a sensible portion of the scum was collected. It is of such strength in perfume that if one drop be rubbed on the palm of the hand it scents a whole assembly, and it appears as if many red rosebuds had bloomed at once. There is no other scent of equal excellence to it. It restored hearts that have gone and brings back withered souls. In reward for that invention I presented a string of pearls to the inventress. Salima Sultan Begam (may the lights of God be on her tomb) was present, and she gave this oil the name of itr-i-jahangiri.'

The drive to Aligarh began well, on the broad, newly constructed Delhi–Agra expressway, which boasts of manicured grass shoulders and plenty of completely legible signage. It carried on, a seemingly endless expanse of smooth, sun-bleached tarmac, until the deception ended quite suddenly after the exit towards Aligarh. All at once, we were back in Uttar Pradesh, among the horse-drawn carts, motorcycles and wildly careening, honking local buses, all on a single carriage road that was but a patchwork of pits, hastily repaired potholes and the odd streak of fresh tar now and then.

The small towns that we now passed were larger, and seemed more populous than the small villages on the drive to Kannauj. There were more shops, bigger concrete buildings and advertisements for educational institutes of various sorts. Most villages were flanked by wheat fields and reservoirs that were unfortunately ringed by slopes of discarded plastic and were possibly also repositories for the sewage of the local populace. Nonetheless, in the spring afternoon light, they looked tranquil.

An hour later, Aligarh announced itself by way of a teeming marketplace. There were pukka shops and a layer of mobile ones in front of them on either side of a narrow street. Food, hardware, general goods, groceries, saris, it was all there. The older part of the city was, typically, a warren of alleys, shabby buildings and houses squeezed in. Most were modern structures, but among them were the more picturesque facades of old havelis, with arched windows and carved jharokas. Their brightly painted wooden doors at street level gave away nothing of the size of the homes that lay behind them. As these thinned out, the newer part of Aligarh, with its wider roads and residential colonies, came into view. By the time I reached my hotel, it was getting to be dusk, and it was too late for me to go see the Aligarh Muslim University or the lock factories for which the city is famous, so I stayed in my room, waiting for the next leg of the journey to begin.

~

I slept fitfully at night, the way one does when the alarm is set for 6 a.m., and had anxiety-fuelled dreams in which I was at an airport shop, contemplating a pre-flight sandwich when I realised with a start that I had neither ticket nor passport with me. I woke before my alarm went off, but in the event, I needn't have bothered. I received an early call from Atul Jain, who asked me to delay my departure to 7.30 a.m. because, even at that early an hour, he was stuck in a traffic snarl on the highway from Kanpur, and now would be late reaching Etah where we were to meet.

The morning light laid bare the town, and my impression of Aligarh was that it was singularly unlovely. It was crowded and grimy, dotted with piles of construction material. As we drove on, the city thinned out and gave way to miles of agricultural land that had been divided into plots with low brick walls, and featured piles of building materials lying around, waiting to be used, and ubiquitous in this region. On either side of the road—although it barely qualified as one, being almost completely broken down—were shops, but the general air was one of somnambulence. Men dawdled on charpoys outside these shops, outside homes, women were nowhere to be seen, and the level of activity was low, except at the brick kilns that appeared at regular intervals, and where men worked under the bright sun and in the ferocious heat of the kiln. We crept along at a snail's pace, the driver focusing hardest on simply avoiding the largest craters in our path.

Some hours (and a mere sixty kilometres later), we stopped at the designated rendezvous point, a petrol pump where I met Jain in his car, and followed him the remainder of the way, off the main highway and onto a narrower road between fields. We stopped at a village, Dahenu, which consisted of a school and a small cluster of brick homes shared by families and livestock.

Getting out gratefully, I was greeted by Jain in a starched white kurta-pajama that bore no evidence of the arduous road trip he had just completed, though mine had left me looking rumpled and feeling loose-jointed. With him was his nephew, recently returned from a perfume school in France—a third generation inducted into the business.

Towards the back of the village was an open space and a small outhouse, next to which the field distillation unit had been constructed. The now-familar rows of copper sills connected to condensers submerged in a rectangular bath were in use, and close by, tractors were unloading sacks of roses; the delicate pink petals being spread out on a sheet to be weighed. The entire operation was being handled by men, and amidst the workers, the tractors, the distilling apparatus and the piles of dung cakes for fuel, the lush carpet of fragrant roses was a glaring incongruity.

I had hoped to see the fields, rosebuds being picked, but not only had I arrived too late (I would have had to leave Aligarh at 3 a.m. in order to be on time), the vast rose fields of my imagination, fragrant and dewy, were not really close to the reality of the Indian rose cultivation system. In India, distilleries and manufacturers get their raw material from local farmers, spread out across fifty to sixty-five kilometres, each of whom tilled his own fields, usually no more than an acre in size. Often, flowers are grown as an adjunct to a main crop to supplement income.

Jain's status as lord of all he surveyed was apparent. He sat comfortably aspill on the white plastic chair, at a vantage point from where he could take in the workers who sat on their haunches, focused on their work. If one of them needed to approach the chair, he did so with caution and the question to be asked was always preceded by a ceremonial dive to touch Jain's feet in tableau of feudal hierarchy.

The typical harvest continues for forty-five days, and during this period, approximately six to eight tonnes of petals—picked early in the morning before they begin to wilt and weigh less—are brought to the field distillery each day to undergo the process of extraction. Work carries on round the clock, and it is labour-intensive and gruelling. Harvesting begins before daybreak between four and five in the morning. The ephemeral and all-important scent of the damascena roses must be caught before the sun comes up and steals it away. Roses that have been under the hot early summer sun lose much of their fragrance to evaporation; the petals become considerably lifeless. Every flower is picked by hand, roses being far too delicate and expensive to be subjected to any sort of manhandling at all, and very often, it is the village women who pitch in and do a large portion of the flower-picking during the harvest season, which is the busiest and potentially most lucrative time for villages. The delicate roses are picked fresh each morning, collected in wicker baskets, which are emptied into sacks and quickly transported to be weighed and distilled.

At the weighing I witnessed, on a cotton sheet spread over the earth, sacks of roses were upturned, their pale pink petals tumbling out and infusing the air around them with that characteristically delicate floral aroma I had first smelt on my visit to the flower fields in Kannauj. Next, they were piled onto a set of scales, an iron tarazu, held aloft by a man who deftly added iron counterweights, and called out a final number. The petals were then transferred to another pile where two men made sure they were spread out and kept moist to prevent them from either fermenting or drying out. The weights, called aloud, were for the benefit of the bookkeeper who sat on a plastic chair with a ledger on a table before him. It was his job to record how much had been brought in and who was the farmer. At the close of the harvest, according to these records kept by him, the farmers were paid an average of Rs 300–400 a day.

~

There are over a hundred species of roses around the world, with many more sub-species, several with a characteristic fragrance. There's a *Rosa moschata* that smells slightly musky, a *desprez* which is fruity, a melon-scented *souveraine* and some that are even reminiscent of cinnamon. Others, like the *Rose de Mai* (from Grasse) and the *Rosa centifolia* are also cultivated for their oil, but it is the *Rosa damascena* which is most widely grown around the world, and the type with the most highly regarded fragrance. In India as well, apart from a small percentage of *Rosa chinesis* grown in Kannauj for gulkand, it is the *damascena* that is cultivated. Indeed, according to Jain, no other variety is commercially sensible, now that rose oil is a big business, unlike in the past where roses had been grown and their oil extracted for personal use by families.

The *damascena* is grown in many countries. Bulgaria, Morocco and Turkey are other, larger producers. The soil, air and water of every region affect the particular fragrance of the rose, much like terroir does to a wine. The Indian one bears its own stamp: a characteristic earthy note. Extraction procedures differ around the world. In India, it is the hydrodistillation process which prevails, as it has for centuries. So while these units are temporary, with one in use and several more being built for the duration of the harvest, the basic parts are the same as they are in the largest distilleries. Copper sills—it is always copper for hydrodistillation, no matter where in the world, due to its non-reactive nature—filled with a mixture of water and rose petals. This mixture is placed on wood and dung-fired brick ovens, attached by coir-covered pipes to copper receivers that are submerged in water to help condense and contain the vapours. The bath for the fourteen receivers in use was the size of a small swimming pool, and it is one person's job to be in there, checking on the receivers to see when they are full—another skill that comes only with experience. Jain had no explanation for how one judges when a receiver needed changing, apart from a benign smile and the mysterious answer that one simply knew, by touch.

A single kilogram of rose oil requires the extraction of between six and seven tonnes of rose petals (four, if the yield has been particularly bountiful). A single copper sill takes forty kilograms of petals, which must float freely in more than twice the amount of water, since coagulated lumps of petals would hinder the process. The water is stirred frequently to prevent just that, and the sills are charged with flowers every five hours. The rose water, in the sills as well the water in the bath for the condensers, is distilled a second time to extract as much of the oil as possible. This is done at night to save time before the next lot of fresh petals arrives in the morning.

The spent petals, leached of their fragrance and colour become a brown mush, bearing no resemblance to their original state at all. Yet, this by-product is too useful to simply discard. The local farmers either collect the residue and bake it into cakes to use as fuel, or mix it with dung ash and then use it to fertilise rose fields, thereby bringing the circle to a close.

By the close of this harvest season, the Pragati field distillery would have produced approximately ten kilograms of rose essential oil, or ruh, valued at Rs 10 lakh per kilogram.

Pragati Aroma uses 75 per cent of the rose oil it produces

in its own products. The remaining 25 per cent of Pragati Aroma's rose oil product is exported to the Middle East and Europe. An additional 100 kilograms of rose itr is made using the same process as the essential oil, differing only in that the bhapkas contain a base of dioctyl phthalate, or DOP, an organic compound that is colourless, odourless, soluble in mineral oil and immiscible in water, and which finds extensive use in the plastics industry. It sounds like an improbable material in a traditional perfume, but in the absence of sandalwood oil, DOP and liquid paraffin are what have replaced it. The use of sandalwood is *na ke baraabar*, next to nothing, according to Jain. The bhapka containing the DOP is left in place for fifteen days before it is judged to have absorbed enough rose essence to qualify as an itr.

The afternoon sun was directly overhead. The tractors ferrying their fragrant cargo from the fields had stopped arriving, but there was still plenty to be done. Across from where we sat in the shade of a neem tree, another row of sills was being readied for action. But I could not stay to watch; it was time I steeled my nerves for the bone-jarring drive back to Delhi via Aligarh. Before I left, I was invited to share the lunch that Jain and his nephew had brought from home. Within the single room of the outhouse were plastic chairs and a wooden table. Half a dozen steel tiffin boxes were laid out, their contents comprising a delicious vegetarian meal, complete with a rich dessert of pistachio-studded halwa.

As I left, I thought of how, if this northern state, unappealing or overwhelming as it sometimes appeared to a solitary traveller, was to have a perfume, it would be a classic one: a scent that represented the earthy beauty of its farms and rich fields through vetiver, which grew wild, and the medieval charm of its crumbling havelis and patina of Mughal-inspired mannerisms through the heady rose. A strong perfume, not necessarily one that would please everyone, but memorable nonetheless.

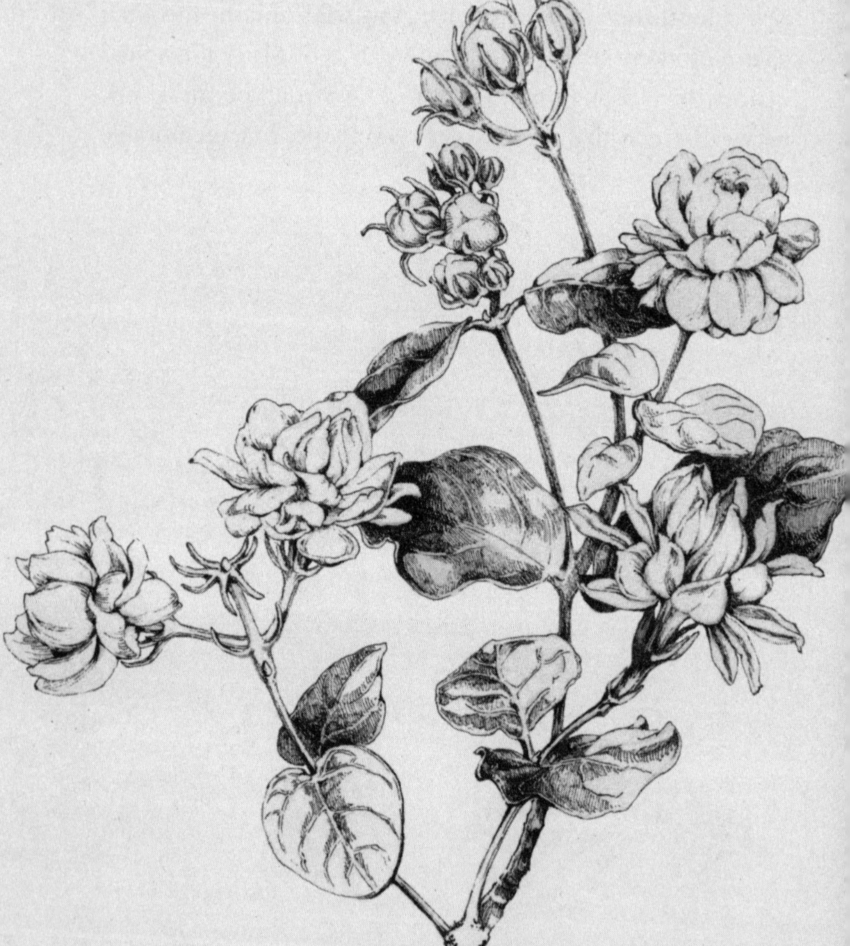

Jasmine

OVER 6,000 KILOMETRES away from home, I was standing very still in the middle of a long supermarket aisle of toothpaste and shampoo. At the head of the aisle, next to the cashier, an armed robbery was underway. Bewildered and jet-lagged, I had left my sturdy suitcase in my rented studio and accepted the landlady's kind offer of a ride to the local supermarket to equip myself for the few short weeks I was to attend a summer school introductory course in perfumery.

The robbery was quicker and less dramatic than any cinematic variation I'd watched, unfolding with efficiency and, surprisingly, absolute silence. A man in all-black moto gear, helmet still on, held a small dark revolver to the head of a petrified cashier. She emptied the till and handed over its contents, which he took and ran out with to his waiting bike. The cashier started crying only after, and was escorted out by two friends for comfort and cigarettes. A minute later, the scattered shoppers, who had (like me) been frozen in their spots, trying to be invisible, stirred to life and carried on with the business of selecting groceries.

The one comforting similarity to home was that the police arrived late.

Since my last trip to Kannauj, my interest in perfumery had only grown. Though I had witnessed but a small aspect of the craft and its practice, it had whetted my interest. There was the world of growers and distillers I'd met, plying their unchanged trade, and also so much more—a deeper knowledge of the oils, their constituent molecules and idiosyncratic properties, the ways in which they changed when blended into compositions and the effects they produced. A very enticing rabbit hole indeed.

I had, after some deliberation, enrolled in a perfumery school in the Provencal French town of Grasse that has been the world capital of the modern perfume industry since the eighteenth century. To study perfumery in Grasse after having explored Kannauj, the 'Grasse of the East', seemed to me the correct thing to do. It provided a pleasing symmetry although I had not counted on the very dramatic way that I had been introduced to it.

There was also the more prosaic fact that the Grasse Institute of Perfumery taught courses in English.

The school was housed in a building that went by the name of Villa Marguerite. It was compact and graceful, with a red-painted fresco that ran along the top. Perched on a hillside neighbouring other picturesque villas, it was a short walk from the town's centre: the Old Grasse, built like a fort with a warren of narrow, interconnecting passages and lanes. Another interesting similarity to its counterpart in India. A bird's eye view would show a green landscape, liberally sprinkled with slivers of azure (mostly swimming pools) and, in the distance, Cannes and the bright blue Mediterranean sea.

None of this was visible from my classroom, which was

located in the basement of Villa Marguerite. It had none of the cozy charm of the offices on the ground floor with their display cases of vintage perfume bottles, alembics and large windows letting in the golden Cote d'Azur light. We had a more utilitarian theme: metal or plastic chairs and tables, shelves neatly stacked with hundreds of bottles of ingredients, rows of electronic weighing scales and a white board. Presiding over it all was Madame Laurence, who had an excellent nose, a dry wit and a thick French accent.

My days were spent in that room diligently smelling paper strips dipped in raw materials both natural and synthetic, learning how to identify, understand and blend them. My nose, which I'd always considered too large, too blunt and too Punjabi, became my most prized feature. Part of the learning process was visits to fields and factories. The first of these was to see the picking of jasmine—a quintessential Grasse bloom.

~

There are approximately 2,000 species of jasmine[35] that can be found growing wild or cultivated, and in every country, the flower is called by various names. In India, I had heard an array of names. Bela, chameli, motia, malli, parijat, raat ki rani, juhi, harshringar: the list was long and poetic, and over time, I had managed to smell and know them all. Motia is beautiful and voluptuous; chameli is sweeter than motia;

35. Ramesh Kumar Srivastava, Shakti Vinay Shukla, Sanjeet Singh Dagar, *Cultivation and Uses of Aromatic Plants*, Lucknow, IBDC Press, 2009, p. 27.

the raat ki rani smells like it's drenched in honey and is my favourite; the harshringar or parijat with its vivid orange centre has a distinctively sulphurous note that is nonetheless quite haunting.

In Grasse, it is the *Jasmina grandiflorum* that is celebrated. The counterpart to the Indian chameli, it is heady, with an oily sweet opulence, sometimes jammy, always with a steady background of funky indoles. These are molecules[36] that aren't the most pleasant smelling (nobody in the perfumery class *ever* wanted to be the first to sniff the strip dipped in a 10 per cent solution of indole) but show up in almost all white flowers and are intrinsic to their overall appeal. Indoles can smell ever so slightly rotten (some would say faecal, even) but to me, they have always smelt very clearly like naphthalene balls, the kind we threw at random into a suitcase of woollen clothes being put away for the next year's winter.

The particular microclimate of Grasse ensures that the jasmine grown here thrives, and contains a special sweetness and a delicacy for which it is prized in perfumery. It is the most important flower of the summer, and in the city is known simply as La Fleur. The Flower. Not much is produced any more, and what is belongs to the big houses, Chanel and Dior. The field I visited was a disappointment, at odds with the status that the Grasse jasmine holds—a scant half-acre,

---

36. Luca Turin, *The Secret of Scent: Adventures in Perfume and the Science of Smell*, Ecco, New York, 2006, p. 61: 'Indole, probably the most unfairly maligned molecule on earth, smells bitter and inky, but is an essential component of all raspy-voiced white flowers.'

sandwiched between an unpaved parking lot and the main road. Still, it employed a dozen pickers, swarthy, sunburnt men and women who made up for the unprepossessing view by being cheerful and enthusiastic. 'It is the best jasmine in *tout le monde*,' one old man declared to me as I stood taking what I hoped were artistic photographs of the tiny white flowers heaped in wicker baskets. I smiled and nodded at the man, but remained sceptical. To begin with, the fragrance of jasmine was not one that I had a great and enduring love for.

Being a 1980s child, encounters I'd had with perfume had often left me feeling overwhelmed. It was not a decade that championed subtlety; the balloon trousers, armour-like shoulder pads, the door-knocker earrings, gravity-defying perms all demanded to be acessorised with scents that could keep up, and the adults I encountered happily obliged. All trends were embraced, often together. The perfumes they wore announced their arrivals and billowed in their wakes. Big florals heavy on the jasmine were popular. *Joy* by Jean Patau was still around, and *Dior Poison*, *Giorgio Beverly Hills* and *Dior Fahrenheit* were all favourites with the uncles and aunties who came to the parties that my parents frequently hosted. Children were not welcome at these soirées beyond brief, obligatory hellos, but we peeped from behind the curtain that portioned the living room from the corridor leading to the bedroom, goggle-eyed as these adults, we knew as parents of friends, transformed into guffawing, dancing revellers. Those parties always smelt of alcohol and huge hothouse blooms laced with sweat, a potent combination that made me wrinkle my nose.

So, jasmine was a note I had learnt to appreciate later, slowly and with deliberation. I marvelled at its immense versatility, but it was a fragrance I could be objective about. Moreover, if there was a jasmine that I felt deserved a lofty status, it was the motia or sambac jasmine, the scent of which almost vibrates with freshness, the green notes and hints of orange flower making it so much more interesting in my opinion than the more classic grandiflorum variety.

There is a popular saying the fine fragrance industry abides by: 'There is no perfume without jasmine.' It makes its way into every fine fragrance, whether a classic floral one, or one that is more modern. Jasmine is always needed. In India, this need becomes strategically valuable because sambac jasmine is arguably India's best-known perfumery export. The flower, despite its unassuming size and appearance, is a colossus in terms of the sway it wields in the fragrance industry. Its history is long and storied, and jasmine, perhaps more than any other Indian perfumery ingredient, carries the immense weight of individual memories, collected over centuries.

Jasmine is grown all over India for its beauty and fragrance. This is also a fact of history, perhaps most notably attested to by the documentation surrounding the stylised and verdant gardens of the Islamic rulers.

Known as Turco-Iranian or Hispano Arab or Medieval Muslim gardens, they were a significant feature of all Islamic lands of the time, from Spain to India. Beautiful, perfumed plants were an integral feature of both the gardens built by the Mughals in northern India, as well as the sixteenth-

and seventeenth-century Deccani gardens of Golconda and Bijapur.[37] Everywhere, these gardens enclosed tanks, or hauz, or housed perennial streams, and were beautiful combinations of man-made architecture and the natural world.

These enclosures were designed to provide a sense of escape, to afford the visitor a space within which reflection (or fantasy) was possible. In these gardens, with their water channels, shaded avenues and beautiful, airy pavilions, fragrance played an important role. By day, the garden was a visual treat full of colour, but by night, it was magical—moonlit and perfumed heavily by the night-blooming tuberose and resplendent jasmine.

Apart from pure pleasure (in itself a major stimulus for the presence of these flowering shrubs in medieval gardens), the significance of a fragranced garden[38] can be appreciated via the theories of Ibn Sina (known as Avicenna in the Medieval Europe). *Materia Medica* by Ibn Sina, perhaps the best-known physician of Islam's Golden Age, provides the outline for the traditional Unani system of medicine, still practised in India and Pakistan.

In this system, human health is dependent on the harmony between the four humours of the body, each of

37. Ali Akbar Husain, *Scent in The Islamic Garden: A Study of Literary Sources in Persiana dn Urdu*, Pakistan, Oxford University Press, 2012, p. 28.

38. Ibid., p. 71: 'Ibn Sina's views on the subject of exhilarating fragrance (Adwiya mufriha), appear relevant to a study about the use of scent in Islamic gardens, because the exhilarating fragrances he writes of are plant-based for the most part, and suggestive, therefore, of a use in gardens.'

which corresponds to the four elements of matter, and a blend of those humours. The most dominant of these dictates a person's general outlook on life, their 'mizaj' or temperament, which was also an indicator for a body's illness and cure, not unlike the 'dosha' in ayurveda.

Additionally, certain 'arwah', pnuema or gaseous components of the body (such as oxygen), considered the source of all life, correspond to the liver, heart and brain, and must be continually nourished. Just as the spirit of the liver is naturally drawn to sweet substances, the brain, according to Unani principles, is bettered by the inhalation of beautiful fragrance.[39]

Beautiful aromatic materials have, of course, been a firm fixture in Indian religious practices for millennia. Early Sanskrit texts like the *Gandhasara*, a treatise on olfactory aesthetics dated to the twelfth century CE, introduced the science of perfumery as one that is pertinent to the essential pursuits of life, namely artha (money), kama (desire), dharma and worship.[40]

---

39. Ibid., p. 72: 'The heart (Plato's "fountain of blood") is said to be fortified with joy and by "gladdening agents" (such as music and good company); and the sensory organs of the brain in particular, are strengthened with fine fragrances (shamumat) and fine vapors (Abkhara-e-latif) ...'

40. James McHugh, *Sandalwood and Carrion: Smell in Indian Religion and Culture*, Oxford University Press, New York, 2012, p. 145: 'So, this treatise, instructive in good and auspicious perfumes is related here by mere indication, [this treatise that] provides for a rite of worship of the gods with incense and auspicious perfumes; makes men thrive; provides the results of the trivarga, and removes one's own misfortune; that pleases kings, and delights the mond of the cultivated lady.'

A passage in the 'Anushasanaparvan', the thirteenth book of the Mahabharata, in which Yudhisthira is instructed by Bhishma on a number of topics, among them that of sacrifice and rituals, also touches upon the use of scent in ritual and religious worship.[41] It is a complex passage, with several threads of narration and dialogue, and within it is a question asked by the lord of daityas: 'What, oh one most knowledgeable of Brahman, is the result of the offering of flowers, incense and lamps?' And the answer: '... since it gladdens the mind and imparts fortune / Therefore [flowers] are called sumanas [good-minded] by those who have performed their deeds well / The pure man who gives sumanas to the gods ... since the gods are satisfied, therefore they are called sumanas.' And further in the passage, it elaborates that, 'One should understand the flowers with pleasant odour to be for the gods / The majorities of thornless trees are white in colour/ The flowers of those ones are constantly desired by the gods.'

The ayurvedic term 'rasa' (which too corresponds in theory to the Islamic 'mizaj') is almost synonymous with the idea of pleasure of all kinds, including, of course, aroma. The seventeenth-century treatise on perfumery, *Itr-e Nauras Shahi*, describes various ways in which to scent the royal bedroom, using flowers arranged in novel ways for maximum olfactory impact.[42] One such description is of a bouquet

---

41. Ibid., p. 223.

42. Ali Akbar Husain, *Scent in The Islamic Garden: A Study of Literary Sources in Persian and Urdu*, Pakistan, Oxford University Press, 2012, p. 81: 'The author of the Itr-e Nauras Shahi describes nine methods

meant for the bedside, which consists of layers of aromatics, including varieties of jasmine along with other flowers.[43]

~

Four months on, it was February once more. The weather in New Delhi was turning amiable, the city's winter shades of sludge broken up by the rows of bright spring flowers on roadside verges and roundabouts. I was planning to head out to flower fields once again, this time to Madurai in Tamil Nadu—a far longer distance than when I had travelled to discover roses, although the four-hour flight would be considerably less arduous than the tooth-rattling drive through UP had been. Once there, I was to meet Raja Palaniswamy, Commercial Director of Jasmine Concrete Exports Pvt. Ltd, which is among the country's best-known makers and exporters of jasmine extract, supplying, among others, Dior. I had read that Francois Demachy, the brand's nose, visited it often on sourcing trips.

Once there, my plan was to visit the sambac fields the morning after, and then to follow the flowers on their journey from field to factory, extractor to bottles.

---

of perfuming the royal bedroom (*khwabgah*), maintaining that each of the nine perfume bouquets (*majumas*) he proposes is composed of the nine, key rasas while retaining its unique identity ... scented flowers, it is suggested, be strung into garlands and hung about the room strewn together with aromatic foliage on the floor and/or placed in platters of silver and glass beside the bed ...'

43. Ibid., p. 82: 'The writer recommends that scented flowers like the champa (Michelia champaca), the mogra (Jasminum sambac), the chambeli (Jasminum auriculatum) and three species of rose, kuza, nivali, and gul-e-lal, be kept together with citrons (turunj) in a glass bowl beside the bed.'

My flight landed in the evening to a welcome 29°C, and I gratefully shed my sweatshirt as I got into the taxi to my hotel. It was a long drive there through busy, commercial streets. Not the town centre, which is the area near the Meenakshi temple, but fairly close. Here, past 7 p.m., all the stores were open and doing brisk trade. Madurai, which has earned itself the tagline 'Athens of the East', was the capital of the Pandya dynasty, and India's most celebrated city during the Classical era. At the heart of the old city stands the Meenakshi Sundareshawara Tirukkoyil, a holy temple dedicated to the goddess and her husband Sundareshwara, an aspect of Shiva who is not the principal deity of the temple. The temple is a pastiche of Dravidian architecture, with a history that goes back 2,000 years and it is also one of the largest in India, occupying sixteen hectares. The temple is also renowned for its twelve distinctive gopuras or towers which dominate the city's skyline.

None of what I saw of the city seemed too far removed from descriptions of Madurai during the first millennium. The Pandyan capital was one of region's most celebrated cities even then, and Tamil texts like the *Maduraikanchi* and *Silappadikaram*[44] note how Madurai stirred awake in the early hours to the sounds of hymns being chanted, how the streets were always busy with the buying and selling of flowers, betel nut, toddy and sweets, and how it was a city that took the pursuit of pleasure seriously. In all of

44. Abraham Eraly, *The First Spring: The Golden Age of India*, Penguin Books, India, 2011, p. 392.

these descriptions, the olfactory stimuli were prominent, and jasmine played a starring role.

~

The following morning, just past dawn, I got into an SUV with Murugan, my escort from Jasmine Concrete Exports, for an hour's drive to the sambac fields. We drove through streets that, much like me, weren't yet fully awake. Past several miles of semi-urban sprawl with its rubbish heaps and goats tied outside small houses, we began to emerge into farmland, and the startling emerald green of paddy fields, interspersed with small fields of flowers in bursts of yellow—marigold and chrysanthemums.

We also passed a half-acre plot growing tuberoses, looking awkward and spindly, their appearance so at odds with the deliciously creamy white scent of their blossoms. A little further, I arrived at Arasumarathupatti (which translates to 'the village of the peepul tree'), a small village around which grew the 300 acres of terraced flower farms I was here to see.

All around was a huge expanse of green, with splotches of colour—either manicured bushes in long rows or fields of hypnotic yellow marigolds and delicate pink oleander, with hills and swaying palms behind them. In some fields, the morning's picking was complete although it was only 6.30 a.m. yet, and in other fields, women were still at work, diligently and gently gathering flowers. It was like stepping into a state tourism board postcard. It was the way I had imagined a flower harvest would look.

In all of it, the sambac jasmine plants were the ones

planted in long, neat rows, the florets on them tiny and brightly white. Unlike the showy flowers that flanked it, the jasmine wasn't all that much to look at—it revealed itself to the nose, not the eye.

The fragrance of fresh sambac jasmine flowers is beautiful, complex and luscious. Sweetly floral with airy green notes at first, but then increasingly voluptuous. Of all the jasmine varieties cultivated for their oil and used in perfumery, the sambac is perhaps the most nuanced—the lush freshness combined with a blast of startling floralcy and the lashings of indole its classic hallmarks.

This is also the reason that sambac jasmine absolute sells at roughly $3,000 per kilogram. Traditionally, it is worn as a ruh, an unblended essential oil, its many inherent layers requiring no other note to buttress it. Whether it is the memory of a mother who wore them in her hair, or that of the smell from a few motia plants carefully tended to in a garden or even just that of a garland bought at a traffic signal and forgotten in the car, the fragrance of the sambac jasmine is one that everyone seems to feel connected to and have a story about. I stayed a while, picking a few buds, taking in the fragrance and the expanse of the peaceful morning, still so clean and new.

On my way back to the hotel, I thought of how witnessing this harvest was like discovering a smaller world. This was the most basic cog the universe of perfumery, set in motion by

the ritual of picking delicate flowers at dawn, flowers whose beautiful exhalations made that universe possible. It was quite miraculous.

After breakfast, I met Raja Palaniswamy. He was as cordial in person as he had been over email, and far more forthcoming with information, of which he had a lot, and patient with questions, of which I had several. He explained that the 300 lush acres I had visited earlier and compared so favourably to the disappointingly small fields in Grasse were also in fact a patchwork of small fields. Each belonged, as had the rose fields in UP, to several hundred individual farmers. The model here was much the same as it was for rose farming in the north. The farmers work the land themselves and harvest the flowers with the help of their families. Those who own farms that are over two acres are the only ones who can, and often do, employ manpower during the harvest season. Pickers are paid between Rs 25–30 per kilogram daily. Everything is sold, usually through agents, to the market where jasmine and tuberose, among several other flowers, are sold wholesale, primarily for use in the temples as garlands and offerings.

'The entire trade is controlled through the flower market,' said Palaniswamy. This became clearer at the Matthuthavani flower market, where we headed to next. We entered a modest-looking building next to the city's bus depot. In no way did the structure outwardly indicate that it was one of the largest, busiest wholesale flower markets in India. Over ten tonnes of blooms are transacted here every day. It was at first glance a scene of wonderful but barely controlled chaos.

A little time spent observing revealed the method. There were rows of numbered stalls that dealt in serious sales, and there were sellers of smaller quantities sitting outside the stalls with little piles of flowers before them, mostly roses, jasmine flowers and buds, chrysanthemums and delicate, pink lotus flowers. There were women making garlands of jasmine to be worn in the hair, deftly weaving the strands of white florets together and arranging them in perfect coils for buyers. Elsewhere I saw huge bales of holy basil and davana, a green herb with an unusually rich, woody, ambery fragrance. I also noticed a constant traffic of men and women carrying huge sacks of fresh herbs and flowers, dripping water as they went. Underfoot was an aromatic sludge of leaves and crushed petals, while all around us the air hummed with a purposeful hubbub.

Trade is the primary purpose of all of that activity. The Matthuthavani market is open from 6 a.m. to 10 p.m. every day (although these are only the official timings—it is entirely possible to buy flowers in large quantities at 2 a.m. if an urgent need arose). The stalls were assigned to agents who bought produce from the farmers. Raja pointed out different varieties of jasmine, and also warned me not to pick up flowers to smell from the heaps on display and then replace them. That, he said, was considered completely uncouth.

Sambac season having not yet begun in earnest, prices were hovering high up near the Rs 700 per kilogram mark, which is easily seven times what it is in high season, when the flowers grow almost faster than they can be picked and supply is plentiful. Curiously, I saw almost only sambac buds in the market, and not the open flower as was the case with the grandiflorum or the *Jasmina flexile* or *Jasmina ariculatum*, all of which were being sold either loose or as garlands, big and small. Raja explained that almost all the sambac produced was used for decoration, garlands and temples, and that the preference in those cases was for buds so they would bloom and last longer. Moreover, buds are easier to pick. During the peak season, pickers usually manage to gather between two and three kilograms of sambac buds a day.

Though jasmine, especially the fragrant motia, is grown all over the country in city parks and on private terraces, the soil and climatic conditions in Madurai suit it best, hence the heft and fragrance of the blooms here. But that is, of course, a commercial concern, and secondary to pleasure which I believe is, along with the well-being of the plant itself, the real reason for flowers.

~

I left the Mattuthavani market with the pockets of my kurta filled with flowers and springs of davana to make my way to the Jasmine Concrete Exports unit and observe the final stage in the flower's journey to pure absolute. On the hour-long drive to Dindigul, once an ancient settlement of political importance, and now an industrial district, I asked Raja about how and when the company had come to be. It was a family-owned business. The first unit had been set up in Coimbatore in 1992 by Raja's father and his brother who up until that point had worked only as electrical contractors. In 2002, they set up a sparsely furnished two-storeyed office, a compact guest house and, of course, the large, high-ceiling building that housed the gleaming steel machinery required to produce the precious sambac absolute.

In order to follow the process chronologically, we started at the back of the building where truckloads of flowers are checked for quality. The minimum weight that the facility accepts is 300 kilograms of a given flower which, after they are unloaded, are spread out on vast carpets that extend across the entire cemented quadrangle, their fragrance filling the space and transforming a corner of the utilitarian factory into pure sensory delight.

Having been sorted, the flowers are then loaded onto the large steel extractor trays, stacked and perforated like idli plates, as Raja put it. The perforations allow the flowers to breathe and stay fresh until the trays are slotted into one of the unit's four extractors, each of which have a maximum capacity of 5,000 litres, which translates to one tonne of jasmine flowers.

Once in there, they are soaked and agitated in food-grade hexane, the primary solvent used for extraction, for a fixed amount of time known as a 'wash'. Sambac requires three such washes in order to dissolve the aromatic compounds in the flower before being moved into an evaporator, which is the next step. Here, as the name suggests, the hexane is carefully evaporated under temperature-controlled conditions, and the result is a solid, waxy block of fragrance: a concrete.

Often, it is this version of the extract that is exported

or sold, since it is easy to package and less delicate than the final product. In the factory, I smelt samples of a few more concretes—beeswax, which smelt like sour, chocolatey honey, and tuberose, which was spicier and more vegetal than sweet floral—before moving on to observe the last step. In the finale, the concrete is mixed with ethyl alcohol, which dissolves all the wax and resins. Once the solvent is removed, it leaves behind an absolute—the most faithful rendition of the essence of a flower.[45]

This mechanised, wonderfully coordinated and orderly process was a new kind of fascinating. The deg and bhapka units of the rose fields in UP had been a lesson in history, but witnessing the processing of jasmine flowers felt like I'd been fast-forwarded to the present where efficiency was paramount and time was the enemy.

It had been a long day and my head felt crammed to bursting with all the information I'd gathered since dawn. Before I left, however, I asked Raja if I could smell a few different jasmine absolutes that the company produces. Jasmine CE has a list of twenty-seven products to their name, including essential oils and absolutes, and though there were several others that I was tempted to digress into (like cardamom, which I find quite hard to resist),

45. When compared to an essential oil—an oil obtained via steam or hydrosteam distillation, as in the case of the traditional method—a floral absolute varies slightly in its chemistry. It contains more of the constituent scent molecules than would be present in an essential oil, giving a richer, truer smelling extract.

I reminded myself that I was there to smell their most important extract.

The absolute of jasmine, or indeed any flower, differs from the essential oil primarily and, most importantly, in quality of scent. Where a comparison is possible, an absolute will always be truer to the original and is usually the preferred extract for use in perfumery. The difference in quality is due entirely to the extraction methods employed. To obtain an essential oil, a flower is distilled through steam, or water and steam, as with rose. For an absolute, there is a more sophisticated solvent-based extraction method employed, which I had just observed first-hand in minute detail.

On the second floor of the office building, in a room with nothing but a table, a few chairs and a tray of samples, I revived myself with a glass of fresh coconut water and readied my nose.

I began by smelling the concrete and absolute of the flexile (taruni) which has a fragrance that is clean and distinctly green, somewhat like dry vegetable stalks. Next was the grandiflorum with its familiar sweetness, slightly fatty and animalic, somewhat like a mothball. Thrown into the mix was the absolute of the tree jasmine ('maramalli' in Tamil), which isn't a jasmine at all, but a tree which produces flowers that have a similar scent when fresh. The extract was pretty, with an edible vanilla note, and very different from the sambac absolute which was handed to me last, and which set off bells in my head, so familiar was it with its burst of white petals and refreshing crispness.

The following morning, I awoke once again to a crescent

moon in a still inky sky, in order to pay an early morning visit to the Meenakshi temple. It seemed only appropriate to pay respects to the goddess, as the temple was really the reason that Madurai and its famously fragrant jasmine flowers were on the world map. The streets around the temple had also been the original site for the flower market, making the distance from floral offering to the deity a short one. Over time, the booming business of flowers had demanded more space and was formally moved to its current location in 2010.

I was driven once more through a city that was slowly coming to life, past coffee houses with people lining up for quick breakfasts and through narrow streets, until suddenly, the car stopped in front of a shuttered chemist. To the right was my first view of the temple. This was the north gate, which is several storeys high and covered with carved figures of animals, gods and demons.

It was 6.15 a.m. I bought a garland of roses, tulsi and tuberose flowers and deposited my shoes with a caretaker before making my way into the temple which was mercifully quiet and peaceful. I walked over the stone floor—worn smooth by the millions of feet that go to and from the temple each day; the temple gets approximately 43,000 visitors on a regular day—and towards the main shrine, passing several smaller ones dedicated to other Hindu deities along the way.

There, the priest at the entrance instructed me to return in thirty minutes. The morning's abhishekam procedure was being carried out, the ritual bath after which the goddess would be ready to receive her devotees. In the meantime, I decided to offer prayers to the Mukkurni Vinayakar, the huge black stone Ganesha outside the Sundareshawar shrine, and visit the Hall of a Thousand Pillars, which houses beautiful stone sculptures and painted friezes.

The ceiling of the temple is decorated with lotus flowers and illustrations from Vedic tales. It is repainted once every twelve years, a fact attested to by the latest artist's name and mobile number, which had been painted into one corner. The temple also encloses a tank, a tranquil mosquito hazard where I hovered until the priests trumpeted the opening of the Meenakshi shrine for darshan.

Finally inside, I stood, first in a line that had already swelled to over fifty people, and waited before a black curtain, while scores of bare-chested priests scurried in and out with trays of flowers, incense and prasadam. Eventually, the curtain was thrown back with a flourish, and everyone shuffled forward, necks craned to get a better look at the inner sanctum. Inside was a dark cave, smoky with incense, echoing with the ceremonial chanting of the priests, their faces lit by the huge incense holders they were waving. And beyond, the dark stone likeness of Meenakshi, resplendent in a sari and covered in garlands, with fragrant jasmine heaped at her feet.

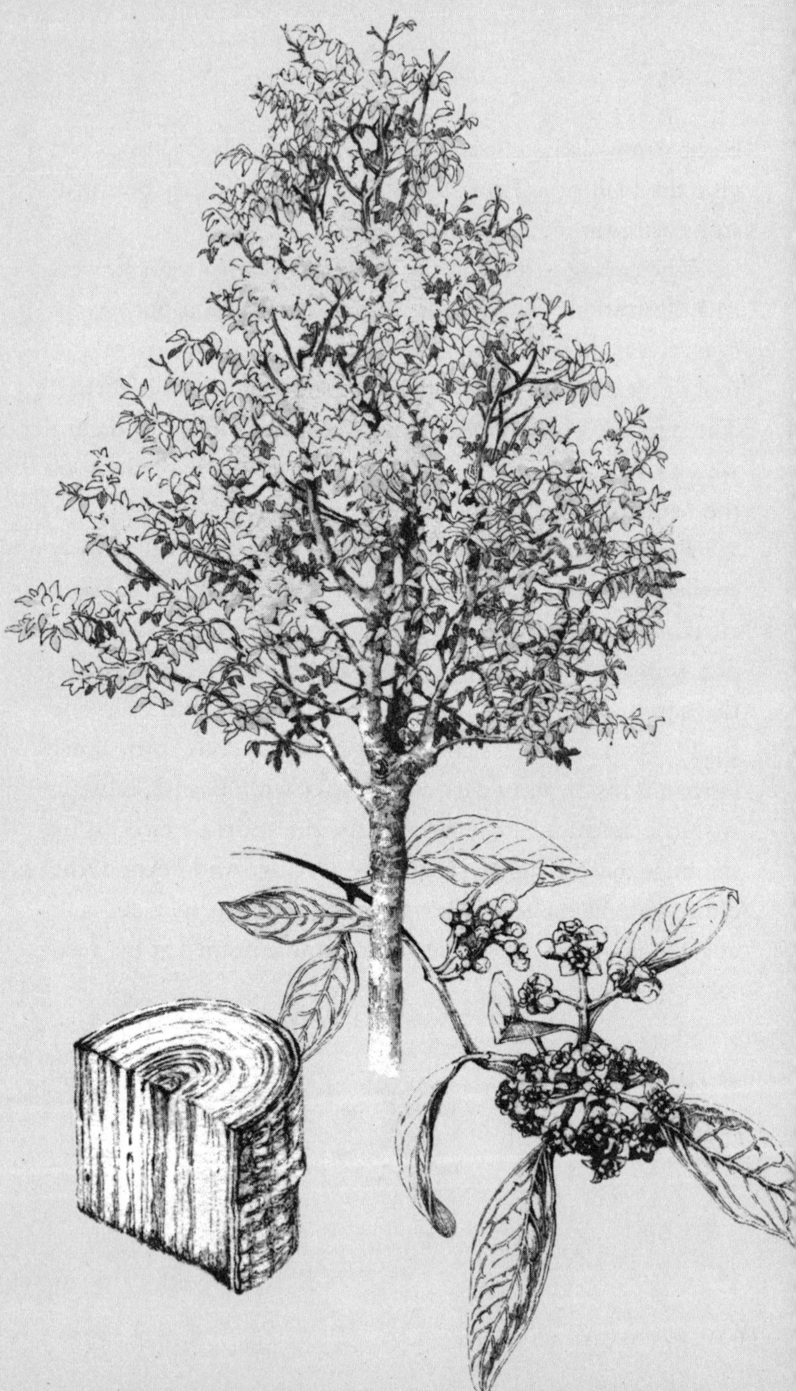

Sandalwood

My parents met each other in 1975 when they were twenty-two years old, and they were married a year later. My mother had just topped the Indian Civil Services examinations, the first woman ever to have done so, and though pleased, was taken aback by the attention it garnered. She was reticent and beautiful, though sadly, she remained unaware of the latter. My father, with his gregarious charisma and movie-star looks, lived on the other end of the spectrum. Solitary pastimes bored him and staying anonymous at any gathering seemed a wasted opportunity. He had a huge imagination that loved to solve problems and—best of all—make up fantastic tales and oddball songs to amuse me with.

When it came to fragrance, however, it was as though my parents' personalities had agreed to a tacit exchange. My mother wore the era's classic perfumes, such as Lancome's *Tresor* or YSL's *Paris*, which mirrored the decade's extravagance. They were assertive and impossible to ignore with their magical, oversized notes of exotic fruits and bright flowers. On the other hand, my father wore pale, cool colognes, and flinched at the woods and ambers used in popular men's fragrances at the time, declaring them to be 'too much'. He appreciated florals as long as they were understated and pretty, and it is a continuous source of delight to me that he has, for decades, worn the classic women's perfume, *L'air Du Temps* by Nina Ricci.

Though I knew his feelings against stronger base notes, I still believed that he would enjoy sandalwood if his introduction to it could be orchestrated correctly. To my mind, his own personality and that of the ingredient were similar enough that there should be a natural affinity: both seemingly tough but unexpectedly gentle. Finally, I decided to compose him a cologne using a small palette of solely natural ingredients—the purest ones have the most evocative smells but lack the strength to last long on the skin. I created a very simple formula, adding no hard edges or animalic notes and gave it to him on Father's Day over a sushi dinner at which I ate the raw fish and he picked the least marine-smelling dish he could. A few weeks later, while visiting him, I saw the bottle, now considerably depleted, among the clutter of others in his bathroom. I asked him if he'd been using it.

'Oh. Yes. I've been using it quite a lot. Actually, it's the only one I'm using now. What all did you put in it?' he asked, a little too casually.

I replied just as casually, 'Oh you know, lemon, orange—stuff I thought you'd like.'

Of course, I strategically omitted mention of the stuff I'd used that I thought he really ought to like: sandalwood.

I have always had a soft spot for the aroma of sandalwood, which contains opposites within itself; it is both hard and soft, sylvan and mildly creamy. In the family of earthy fragrances, it stands out for being the most faceted, the least austere. The popular saying in perfumery, that there could be no perfume composed without jasmine, was one that I thought applied better to sandalwood, and I gravitated toward perfumes that used it in doses large or small.

There had been a brief time in my life, though, when the smell of sandalwood smoke had been an unwelcome one. A single summer in which I had taken to burning sandalwood incense after sundown, and during the course of which my dog died. I felt the loss keenly, and for weeks the rooms of my house seemed only to be full of an unnatural silence and that sweet, woody scent filling every corner. With time, the association changed from being one of sorrow to that of comfort, and comfort is what the scent of sandalwood continues to speak of to me. Perhaps this preference was one that I was predisposed to, even hardwired for, coming as I did from India, where for centuries it had been celebrated and used to scent people's daily lives. What *was* it about sandalwood?

The history of the sandalwood tree lays bare just how valuable it is, and always has been. It was central to life at court, to commerce, to religious ritual, genteel life and, most importantly, to the imagination via which it finds mention in poems and epics. The sandalwood in question was usually the heartwood of the *Santalum album* tree, native to the dry and deciduous forests of the Deccan in southern India—the Sanskrit word 'chandana' is thought to have Dravidian origins.[46] Mentions of sandalwood in traditional Indian texts

---

46. James McHugh, *Sandalwood and Carrion: Smell in Indian Religion and Culture*, Oxford University Press, New York, 2012, p. 184: 'The Sanskrit word *candana* is likely of Dravidian origin, possibly related to a term cantu meaning "*daub*, rub into a paste; sandalwood (paste)" suggesting that this material came from, or passed through, a Dravidian-speaking area prior to being introduced into Sanskrit.'

predate the Rig Veda. It makes appearances in the 'Nirukta' and the 'Mahabhasya', both dated to around the second and third centuries BCE.

In the classical Hindu epics, the Ramayana and Mahabharata, sandalwood makes frequent appearances, most often in the form of a paste, which kings and nobles smeared on their chests for its cooling properties, its fragrance and as a conspicuous marker of affluence.[47] A description in the Mahabharata of Yudhisthira's bathing ritual mentions his 108 bath attendants washing him with sandalwood-scented water. The last step of the ritual required Yudhisthira to smear himself with sandalwood paste and wear a garland, before moving on to prayer. In the same epic, at another point in the proceedings, his brother Bhim's famous weapon, the mace, is rubbed with sandalwood paste as adornment.

The ancient Indian treatise on statecraft, the *Arthashastra*, talks of the importance of sandalwood, among other aromatics, in the royal treasury. The text lists several different variants classified by colour and, of course, fragrance as well by the important ayurvedic quality of being able to combat heat.[48] For this reason, sandalwood also gets an important place in medical texts like the *Dhanvantariyanighantu* (1000–1100 CE). Here, the chapters are divided by groups of various

47. Ibid., p. 186.

48. 'Light, unctuous, not dry, smearing oil like ghee, of pleasant smell, suitable for the skin, mild, not fading, tolerant of warmth, absorbs great heat, and pleasant to touch–these are the qualities of sandalwood (candana).'

materials of medical value, and all fragrant substances come under the banner of chandanivarga, or sandalwood.

In 2014, soon after that fateful summer—the first time I'd become so aware of the presence of a fragrance—my curiosity about sandalwood was piqued. I attempted to read about it in a Government of India report published in 1994, concerning the production of sandalwood in India. After a few attempts at wading through statistics and details of prevalent diseases and fungi, I'd grasped very little and had fallen asleep twice in the library. So I decided that I needed a livelier way to have things explained to me, a live demo of sorts, and planned a visit to the Institute of Wood Sciences and Technology in Bangalore.

Its discovery came as a surprise to me, but even in the city, few appeared aware of the presence of this institute. Twenty-five acres of calm and verdure in the middle of the frenetic metropolis seem hardly possible, and yet, there it was. As it happened, my week-long trip coincided with Van Mahotsav, a day to celebrate forests, and upon arrival, I was very quickly co-opted by the institute's staff into digging small pits to plant sandalwood saplings. Others planted in previous years stood nearby, looking gangly and adolescent. Dr V. Ramakantha, the director of the institute, was a dedicated botanist, and when he spoke on the subject, he became impassioned.

Trees native to the Western Ghats were his particular interest and it was his dream to see them proliferate and become favoured over the invasive, foreign species that he viewed as interlopers. These intruders include the gulmohar, a species I had assumed was entirely native, given how well-loved and oft-planted it is. As it happens, the gulmohar comes from Madagascar. At the institute, as part of some well meant but sweeping changes, Ramakantha had recently cut down an old gulmohar tree whose spreading roots were causing damage. There had been protests when tree-huggers got wind of the news.

During the few days I spent there, I discovered that the subject of wood in general, and native sandalwood in particular, was one that everyone at the institute felt strongly about. I spent mornings meeting scientists who explained that the preferred norm for *Santalum album* trees that grew in forests was to allow them to flourish, and then perhaps to harvest them when they were a few decades old, when the trees were rich in oil. However, plantation owners nowadays are less inclined to be patient, or ignore the profits to be gained, and harvest trees once they are fifteen years old. I saw samples of precious sandal heartwood—neat, pipe cleaner-sized cylinders that were obtained using a two-foot long, mean-looking steel borer. These borers are able to inform analysts of a tree's expected oil yield and genetic traits. I smelt pure Mysore sandalwood oil and understood what set it apart scientifically: a very high proportion of a molecule, santalol, which is responsible for the characteristic scent. In layman's terms, a beautifully gentle, woody and sweet fragrance that was singular.

In the afternoons, I returned to the campus guest house for lunch, and for some space to ruminate on all the information I'd gathered. Each day, lunch was followed by a spell of rain, which seemed to me the most fitting occurrence in this unusual oasis. The warm showers rendered the greenery brighter, lusher. The fat drops of water rhythmically dripping from plate-sized leaves of decorative palms onto the concrete below became the loudest sound. A scant twenty minutes later, sunshine again. And then, a cacophony of birds, sun-dappled trees—the atmosphere of a wet forest.

From Ramakantha, I heard the story of a poaching attempt that had taken place on the campus. It had all the makings of an urban legend. At home, asleep with the rest of his family, the professor had received a panicked call from the security guard. Men armed with knives and unholy intentions had come for the sandalwood trees. An altercation had ensued and their attempt eventually thwarted, but poachers are, of course, relentless and over the years, the losses for the institute became distressingly high. Poachers wiped out two field stations, each of which was a protected copse of twenty-five trees that were clones grafted using tissue from the finest *Santalum album* specimens. The trees had been carefully nourished with the hope that they would be propagated and used eventually to resuscitate South India's reputation as the source of the finest sandalwood. Everything had been carefully planned, except perhaps the security.

The laws in Karnataka regarding the protection of sandalwood are stringent, but the reality tends to fly in the face of those. Campuses that host the trees are regularly targeted by poachers, even within Bangalore, where, as recently as two years ago, thirty trees had systematically disappeared from a university campus,[49] making it hard to not draw conclusions about collusion with law enforcement.

'There are still many Veerappans, small small,' the professor said resignedly and, unfortunately, he was correct.

Veerappan. I remembered the name splashed across in newspapers I'd barely glanced at as a teenager in boarding school. At the time, the peculiarity of the entire saga had been lost on me. Koose Muniswamy Veerappan, a legendary forest brigand, had achieved the dubious distinction of being renowned for sandalwood poaching, becoming a household name in the late 1990s in India. He had been at large in the forests of the Western Ghats between 1970 and 2004 when he was killed. In that time, he had terrorised the police and the border security forces in Karnataka, Kerala and Tamil Nadu, managed to poach over 10,000 tonnes of sandalwood, wiping out entire forests' wealth of the venerable and ancient trees. The anguish of such ecological destruction was subsumed by the details of the many dead bodies he left in his wake. Nabbing him took twenty years, and cost the government over a billion dollars and much loss of face. In a typically Indian twist, the final straw had been Veerappan's kidnapping of the Kannada movie idol Rajkumar, soon after which he was shot in a massive manhunt.

The demand for sandalwood in Middle Eastern and South Asian countries was (and remains) unrelenting, and

---

49. 'Sandalwood trees need protection', *Deccan Herald*, 17 November 2021, https://www.deccanherald.com/opinion/second-edit/sandalwood-trees-need-protection-1051853.html.

poaching lucrative for those who could evade the authorities. Veerappan had been doing brisk trade with other nations, or so the story goes. In doing so, he knew perhaps that he was only following an ancient tradition.

Nineteenth-century German philosopher Georg Hegel,[50] before he dismissed Indian philosophy altogether, conceded that India's treasures were fabulous enough that seeking them out was the moving force of Western history. The list of what he considered our treasures is compact, and features incense and woods prominently, alongside the obligatory diamonds and pearls. India had been a central part of the trade network that connected the globe since the time of the Indus civilisation, which traded with the Middle East by land and sea.

Over 10,000 tonnes of sandalwood! In the entire torrid tale of Veerappan, that was the one statistic that haunted me. I had seen sandalwood trees, a few wood chips and samples and had smelt the oil. My imagination didn't extend to visualising it in tonnes; it seemed entirely too decadent. Not to mention improbable, all things considered. There was just one place that I knew of where, with some luck, such a sight could be within the realm of the possible—Mysore.

Like so many Indian cities, it is layered with history and

---

50. Georg Wilhelm Friedrich Hegel, *The Philosophy of History*, Dover Publications, New York, 1956, reissued in 2004, p. 142: 'From the most ancient times downwards, all nations have directed their wishes and longings to gaining access to the treasures of this land of marvels, the most costly which the Earth presents; treasures of Nature—pearls, diamonds, perfumes, rose-essences, elephants, lions, etc.—as also treasures of wisdom.'

with the legends of great rulers and kingdoms past, but unlike the others, Mysore exudes a sense of serenity rather than one of barely contained chaos. It makes a fitting location for the 100-year-old Karnataka Soaps and Detergents Limited (KSDL), the oldest sandalwood distillery in the country and makers of the famed Mysore Sandalwood Soap, which, as of 2006, has its own geographical indication tag. Established in 1916 by Maharaja Krishnaraja Wodeyar, ruler of the state of Mysore until his death in 1940, the factory still inhabits its original Indo-Saracenic-style building. It is hard to imagine a more graceful setting for what could be considered a mundane, industrial process.

Except, of course, with an ingredient as lofty as sandalwood, nothing is ever mundane.

KSDL is a government-owned and -operated factory, a public sector undertaking since 1980. Despite its soothing setting and historic significance, you could easily drive past it and not notice or take anything away from the place, which is what most people do. Within it though is a portal to another time—a slower pace commemorative of natural bounty and new-found industry.

The steam distillation process that sandalwood and other woods are subjected to in order to extract oil is one that I was familiar with. The wood is cut into logs, the heartwood separated further into pale, fragrant billets which are then fed into a woodchipper, a machine that is true to its name. The chips of wood are further broken down in a disintegrator to a coarse powder, and then subjected to superheated steam in stills to coax out the oil. After that, it goes to a condenser, and next into a collection pot that is manually, and carefully, skimmed of the oil. The oil is further filtered, once in a basic separator to get crude oil, and finally again in a dry vacuum machine, after which emerges the golden, gorgeously scented oil that we know.

The sapwood, or outer layer, that isn't distilled is separated, and this too is auctioned annually via the forest department. When I visited, there were thirty tonnes stacked high across an entire meandering corridor, waiting to to be claimed. Bids came from across the country, I was told, and the wood was used sometimes for handicrafts but most often for funeral pyres of the rich. Tonnes of sandalwood going up in smoke, quite literally.

Here, however, the distillation of the heartwood was rendered more charming by the space in which it was taking place. The high-ceilinged entrance hall had pigeons roosting in the rafters, bare stone floors that had been swept clean, a loft with a delicate wooden balustrade and a hand-painted flowchart illustrating the extraction process. On display were three large pieces of antique sandalwood, one of them a root exquisitely gnarled and striated. A set of dark blue double doors to my right led to the storeroom, which was kept locked.

What could be more inviting? As someone who'd grown up on a steady diet of mystery stories and in a strict boarding school with various areas of no admittance, locked doors (painted blue, no less) were hard to resist. Whatever lay behind them was almost always worth investigating, and rarely disappointing.

I imagined it as a kind of Ali Baba's cave, piled high with sandalwood and perfumed. And I was not disappointed. The storeroom was cavernous, stretching to the length of several rooms with the same high ceilings and sense of peace as the rest of the building. Everywhere were stacks of wood—beautiful, rare and valuable sandalwood, separated into graded lots. The wood, for the most part, came from forest departments across South Indian states. I stood next to 6,000 kilograms of Class I wood from the Shimoga district. This cache had been collected from trees that fell naturally as well as those felled by poachers who had been unlucky enough to be caught.

Small farmers who sold sandalwood trees that had been on their property accounted for a smaller proportion of the store's riches. Sometimes, the farmers got lucky. As a case in point, I was shown a few hundred kilograms of heartwood, all of it from a single tree that had earned its owner Rs 35 lakh. Other times, farmers felled their sandalwood trees too soon, but preferred to earn less from the sale than face the possibility of poachers on their land as the tree grew older. At that moment, there were approximately seventy tonnes of sandalwood in the storeroom. I stood still, looking around me in awe, trying to commit the scene to memory, taking in the sights, sounds and smells of such an exquisite space.

I had lucked out and arrived on what was the year's last day of distillation. The next day, the stills were to be emptied after having been operational for the last seven months. They wouldn't be used for another eight months, when the distillation process would begin all over again. I found it fascinating that the stills I saw in the present day had first been fired nearly a century ago when the Maharaja first hit upon the idea of profiting from the sumptuously scented soaps he used and often gifted to visiting dignitaries. At its peak, the company operated twenty-four stills, and produced up to 30,000 kilograms of oil, much of which was exported across the world and used in the original formulations of perfumes such as Guerlain's iconic *Samsara*, which is a beautiful ode to Mysore sandalwood. The numbers seemed impressive to me, having only previously seen sandalwood oil in tiny vials, but the harsh truth is that the factory, like the entire Indian sandalwood industry, had seen better times.

Today, KSDL produces less than a fourth of the amount it did thirty years ago. The 2,500-odd kilograms of oil that it does produce annually is for captive consumption by the company for its own products, prime among which continues to be Mysore Sandal Soap, which proudly boasts of pure sandalwood oil among its ingredients.

The reasons for this decline are multifarious and saddening. The forests of the Western Ghats, with their once-abundant population of sandalwood trees, have been systematically denuded of them by poachers. This accounts for 15–20 per cent of the loss—less than I had imagined. The government, which until recently had had absolute ownership of every sandalwood tree on the land, has been reaping them too.

Trees are a law and a universe unto themselves, with secret lives and a dimension of time vastly different from the one that humankind operates on. Slow to grow, sandalwood trees look spindly even after two decades, and are resolutely unconcerned with matters of harvests and oil yields. The loss of such fragrant forests is an immense one, and trying to replenish them, a Herculean task. Which isn't to say that attempts to do just that are not being made. Between 2002 and 2014, the Forest Department rules across the South Indian states were amended to allow private ownership of sandalwood trees. Saplings are widely distributed and cultivation is encouraged, even as far north as Gujarat, which barely edges in to what is considered the sandalwood belt.

Results will be slow to arrive. Meanwhile, there are always man-made alternatives—synthetic molecules that can mimic the smell of sandalwood (many of them, superbly well), or at least approximate it, in the absence of the real deal.

After two days of walking about the factory, practically soaking in the ambient smell of sandalwood that was as much a part of the place as its machines, I couldn't leave without taking some back with me, and not just as a memory. From the KSDL factory shop, I purchased five grams of pure Mysore sandalwood oil. It came in a simple steel bottle, painted in black, placed in a felt pouch. Back home, I put it away in an old wooden cigar humidor along with a few others I'd secreted away—perfumes I had made, or samples of ones I loved. Every now and then, I open the bottle for a sniff. It is reassuring. The sweet, creamy smell always unchanging, as comforting as the first time I'd come to be hooked on it.

When dealing with a wood as rare as *Santalum album*, any waste is considered blasphemous. Every kilogram of oil produced leaves behind disintegrated, powdery wood. Extract a few hundred kilograms of oil and you get entire rooms full of what is technically called 'de-oiled spent powder', raked into sweet-smelling brown hillocks. This residue cannot be simply discarded as it contains still a tiny percentage of oil that could not be coaxed out by steam, and thus, it is given a new lease on life as perfume in its original form and intent: incense.

Beautiful fragrances have an intangible, compelling attraction, and for centuries, perfumers have been willing to forage for root, bark and flower in order to somehow get to their fragrant hearts, and then perhaps be able to compose something marvellous; a scent sublime enough for the mortal world and the imagined realms above it. The beautiful and unseen scents of natural substances have long been assumed to contain the presence of god. The first use of perfume was always to pay tribute to this higher force, the fragrances believed to be powerful enough to travel across realms that humans, in mind or body, could not. In other words, the aromatic smoke of incense was believed to have the power to open doors between the worlds.

In India, incense-making is a kind of cottage industry, often run by women, who hand-roll sticks and sell them to supplement the household income. The ingredients are fairly basic: bamboo sticks, powders of charcoal as well as something called 'jigit' (possibly acacia) which acts as a binder, and sandalwood or other assorted dried herbs and flowers. That is the traditional recipe. A paste is kneaded and given time to develop its fragrance, then deftly rolled and left to dry. The entire process is controlled by the incense-maker's finely tuned sense of time and smell.

Here at the factory, handmade incense had been phased out over thirty years ago. Pre-made batti sticks were now bought from Vietnam. At the factory, these were dipped into vats of perfume and diethyl phthalate (DEP), a chemical solvent, and then sent on their way. This, I personally thought, was an unfortunate development, given that traditional incense was becoming fashionable again elsewhere in the world, precisely for being handmade and somewhat imperfect.

There was also a smaller room—also with a high ceiling and similarly airy but far more ramshackle, with bits of machinery and tubs of black paste and sheets of tarpaulin lying around—dedicated to the making of incense cones.

The ingredients remain the same. The still-fragrant sandalwood powder is mixed with acacia, charcoal, water and a synthetic perfume (a thoroughly unnecessary and almost disrespectful step, in my opinion), before being poured in to one end of a machine that, with hypnotic rhythmic regularity, pressed out the small cones. These are dried in the sunlight over two days (that explains the tarpaulin sheets draped all over) before being packed into boxes of twenty. Each box is sold for Rs 20 in the market, and Rs 18 if purchased at the factory shop. The cones make their way into almost every household and shop in the city, where they are burnt for morning prayers, the sweet sandalwood scent rising to fill the room.

The history of sandalwood, its movement across the globe, is like an opera. The picture, as I stepped back and saw it, was pleasingly symmetrical. Here is a fragrance that has never fallen out of favour, always revered, coveted and fought over. Ancient India held the olfactory sense in high regard.

Perfume was no small matter then, just as it isn't now. Mysore sandalwood has always signified luxury, comfort and a quiet satisfaction to the wearer. Some things just don't change.

Saffron

Sometimes, I think about all the places that fragrance takes me to. Many of them are just in my wild imaginings: unknown places, familiar ones lost to time, huge landscapes or just small nooks; I visit them all. And many other places are very much in the physical, prosaic realm. Though where I live is made up of a multitude of scents, to understand the rarest of them calls for travel to some of the further reaches of the country. Which is how I found myself in Srinagar in November, in a season poised between a brilliant earth-toned autumn, still generous with sunshine and impressively blue skies, and a sullen winter with morose clouds, chilling wind and rain. I was chasing the saffron harvest—something I'd very nearly given up hope of seeing.

Spice and, by extension, perfume have played a central role in the history of the subcontinent; India was routinely classified in Western medieval discourse as the most likely location for 'paradise', a source of exotic and valuable aromatic materials.[51] In practical terms (as in, those of long-distance trade), India was always rich in all the materials that made up the canon of ancient perfumery. Along with

51. Paul Freedman writes in *Out of The East* of how 'before the partial opening of Asia to Western eyes in the late thirteenth and early fourteenth centuries, the place of India was close to that of the earthly paradise'.

sandalwood, agarwood and a few others, saffron was foremost a marker of wealth, value, beauty and, more simply, pleasure.

Within the country as well, there has long been a tradition of regional associations with aromatics that were well known and celebrated, in much the same way as regional cuisines, ornaments or styles of dress were. In a text dating around 900 BCE,[52] a manual for poets called the *Kavyamimamsa*, author Rajasekhara proposes a geographical classification of India, along with the characteristics of each area, the cities within them and the products from the area, including the prominent fragrant materials—useful details for the benefit of poets who may use them to more realistically describe a region. Beginning from the east, beyond Varanasi, he moves clockwise. To the south, rich in sandalwood, to the west, from where comes guggul and, finally, to the north,[53] which encompasses Saka, Hana, Kamboj and Turuska, and is known for cedar and saffron. The spice was so synonymous with its area of origin that, in texts and formulas, it was interchangeably referred to simply as 'Kasmira' or 'Kasmirjanma'.

Kashmir, to one who encounters it primarily via the national news, seems like a forbidding place. The world's

52. James McHugh, *Sandalwood and Carrion: Smell in Indian Religion and Culture*, Oxford University Press, New York, 2012, p. 171.

53. Ibid., p. 172: 'Finally Rajasekhara tells us the characterstics of the northern region, beyond Prthudaka, a region including amongst other places, Saka, Huna, Kamboj, Bahlika, Vahlava, Turuska, Barbara etc. The products of this region are pine, deodar cedar, grapes, saffron, yak-tail fly whisks, antelope skins, *Sauvira* antimony (for kohl), rock salt, *vaidurya* gemstones, and horses.'

most heavily militarised zone. Beautiful and hostile. Making a trip there involved a certain level of trepidation and much well-meaning advice from others about exercising caution and how best to navigate the Srinagar airport with its distressingly high number of security checks. Happily, as my flight there was an early one, I was too sleepy to be nervous and, on the whole, too excited about this visit to a state I had not been to since 1984 (a visit I've discounted entirely on account of having been a toddler at the time) to worry. At the Srinagar airport, arrival poses no hiccups, but just as I was wheeling my case toward the exit, a security guard stopped me. For a beat, I was worried, but as it happened, all she wanted to detain me for was not wearing a sweater. 'Don't just hold on to it, put it on. You are in Kashmir now!' she admonished, and I complied sheepishly before carrying on, well-clad, out of the terminal and into a clear, bright day.

This was also the first of my perfume trips (or so I'd come to think of them) during which I would not be absolutely alone, a thought that buoyed me and added to the excitement of being there. Though I had arrived solo, I had a Kashmiri friend in the city who was visiting home and was willing to be a helpful accomplice.

Army personnel, sandbag barriers, guns and barbed wire were all still an inescapable and sobering part of the landscape, but even so, all that drab olive and khaki was overshadowed by the fall foliage putting on its annual display. The chinar trees, synonymous with Kashmir, were especially beautiful. Tall and graceful, their flourishing canopies alive with red, gold and saffron leaves, they left me slack-jawed. Doubtless,

I am gauche—a city girl for whom natural beauty is usually seen corralled in parks. In Kashmir, as it casually asserted itself at every turn, paying no heed to less appealing man-made structures around it, I was in a state of constant awe, trying to take it all in: the vast blue skies and crisp air, the peaceful lake, the many bridges over the city's waterways and the unique views, so different from those of any city I've been to. It was a while before I finally arrived at the family-run guest house, complete with creaky wooden floors and bukhari heaters, where I was to be staying at for the week.

The following morning, with the weather leaning towards a spell of winter rain, we set off for Pampore with our taxi driver, Javed. Pampore is an important site for saffron cultivation and recognised as a Globally Important Agricultural Heritage System by the United Nations for its agricultural and historical significance. We took the old highway route, no longer used for heavy traffic and now flanked on either side by the markers of what appeared to be a construction boom. Everyone, it seemed, was building a house and many, it further appeared, had abandoned the plan at some intermittent stage. There were houses with raw cement walls, missing roofs and windows all along the way. Stonecutters and welders had set up stations, and construction debris was everywhere, in sharp and dismaying contrast to the natural setting of the rushing Jhelum and the ochre tones of autumn.

After a bit, we reached the main chowk which, like the overcast sky, looked leached of colour—all muddy puddles and men in long, grey pherans, a kind of northwest frontier imagery that was new to me. Here we met Rakib Ahmad, the saffron grower, who joined us and directed the driver off the main road, past less inhabited areas and up towards the fields.

Locating a grower who was willing to be interviewed in person was perhaps the biggest challenge of this journey, and I was thankful for my Kashmiri friend and the local network he could mine in order to help me. The questions he had answered on my behalf earlier had unnerved me a little. Why was I interested? Was I a man or a woman? Was I Muslim? Still, Rakib had made no objections in the end, and I was grateful.

There has been a motif that runs through every flower field that I have visited in the course of research thus far—a mismatch between any expectations I hold and the reality I am presented with. This was no different. In my imagination (and also on Google images), saffron fields stretched as far as the eye could see, a vivid purple on all sides, dotted with women bent over, carefully plucking the crocus blooms and placing them into straw baskets. In reality, however, though the tilled earth did span quite far and wide, the flowers were fairly sparse, just dots of bright colour against the deep brown land. Most had been picked already, some were still to bloom. The two women I saw picking flowers in the distance were only using paper bags. The scene seemed diminished.

In Kashmir, saffron bulbs are planted in August. Rakib explained to me that his fields, like most here, are tilled and prepared without chemical fertiliser, relying instead on manure and organic matter. On the twenty hectares he farms, he has planted approximately two tonnes of bulbs.

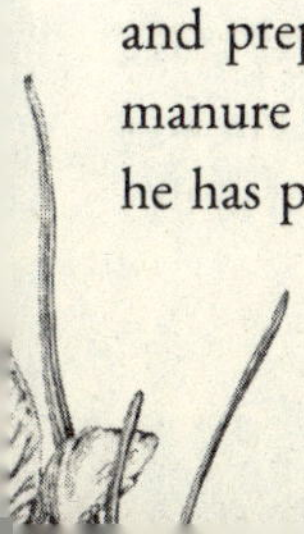

Saffron, or *Crocus sativus*, is a geophyte—it grows from underground corms (or mother bulbs), and one corm produces several more, which need to be dug up and divided from time to time so they're not cramped or rotting underground. This necessary bit of human intervention is also why saffron isn't really seen growing in the wild, and why the propagation is as labourious as every other step in the harvest. Knowing when the separation needs to be done is not an exact science. When I asked Rakib how he could tell the correct time, he laughed politely: 'Well, the farmer always knows about his own crops, but I would say around seven years is enough time.'

The fresh bulbs are then planted in a new bit of land, thus increasing cover, and harvested in the fall. Flowering is triggered by the drop in temperature, and each corm develops between one to four flowers that have the characteristic mauve or lilac shade, often with a violet stain at the throat. Unusually for crocuses, saffron flowers have a fragrance. An earthy honey-and-violet one—a siren song to pollinators. Within the petals are the three stamens, as well as the three stigmas that are divided into terracotta-hued strings—these are the prized saffron threads.

'We usually begin harvest by 24 October,' Rakib added, which was a most precise date, I thought.

Of course, when it comes down to the stark realities, the business of saffron cultivation is nowhere near as precise a matter. For the past several years, yields have been declining steadily and profits along with them. Practically every year, newspaper articles debate whether it is possible to save Kashmiri saffron and, most often, the conclusions are not heartening. Rakib mentioned that, for the number of bulbs planted, his expected yield would be over 500 kilograms of flowers, which in turn ought to equal ten kilograms of saffron. However, this year, like the one before, he had to make do with three kilograms of saffron.

The primary problem is that of irrigation. Depending entirely on nature is rife with risk, and rainfall over the last several years has been erratic, as has snowfall, which means that the ground does not retain enough moisture. Excessive rainfall in some years during the flowering phase caused crop failure, as did the floods in 2014. The ill effects of climate change are felt here keenly.

The government has made attempts to address the situation, notably through the National Saffron Mission set up in 2010, with a budget of over Rs 400 crore and an aim to improve soil health, build a network of tube wells and sprinkler systems, and offer financial support to the farmers, all of it hopefully culminating in increased production. The results of the mission have been lacklustre. In its first five years, the government managed to dig less than half of the 109 wells it had planned, most of which are not functional. They also tried introducing more modern methods for cultivation, but either from a lack of preparatory education, a resistance to change or some mix of the two, nothing really caught on. The result is that growing this rare spice has become unprofitable and riddled with risk for farmers, many of whom have switched to other crops or have sold part of their land.[54]

---

54. Mudassir Kuloo, 'Fading Flavour: As saffron production declines in Kashmir, farmers switch to apple, almond, walnut and vegetables', *Gaon*

Though technically this is prohibited—the land earmarked for saffron-growing is prized—it occurs nonetheless. In fact, a few years ago, the government acquired over 100 acres of it to build the police headquarters on.

As I left the field to follow the saffron onwards, one of the women gave me a handful of the brilliantly purple flowers to take with me. I reflexively raised them to my nose and inhaled. I thought of how I know this smell, not just because I work with it and know what it can do, technically, in composition, but of how I know this scent in my heart, in my bones.

Saffron is the smell of comfort. It's the smell of don't-worry-everything-will-be-fine-here-eat-this, the smell of the sweet, milky and spiced phirni that my grandmother made. As a child growing up across cities, moving homes frequently, there had been something of a gap in my life by way of traditional family trimmings. In my family, the rule was that adults went to work, and children made up their own entertainment and tried to stay out of trouble. Large extended family holidays or cobbled-together religious rituals were sporadic at best. After my parents' divorce and my subsequent move to boarding school, they quietly fizzled out. Any that survived, I credit squarely to the efforts and influence of my paternal grandmother, my dadi, who was every bit the reigning matriarch during her lifetime. She was a formidable lady, unusual in some ways. She'd had a liberal

Connection, 30 December 2020, https://en.gaonconnection.com/fading-flavour-as-saffron-production-declines-in-kashmir-farmers-switch-to-apple-almond-walnut-and-vegetables/.

college education, rare for a woman of her generation, and, even when married, largely declined to cook, citing (quite rightly) tedium as the reason. But she had also lived through Partition, seen much of the horror it unleashed and held to the belief that family was of paramount importance. Everyone in it was required to love and show up for one another or, at the very least, make a very convincing show of it.

My own relationship with her hadn't always been a smooth one. The gap in our views, wide enough already from being two generations apart, grew deeper as I grew older. She would often seek me out to talk about the rift between my parents, while I tried to avoid the sore topic as far as possible and just get on with navigating my fraught-enough teenage life. She, like most grandmothers, equated love with food and was never satisfied by the quantities I ate, but I had discovered that being even slightly overweight in an all-girls boarding school was basically akin to existing in a constant state of wretchedness. I wanted nothing but to fit in, be thin and indistinguishable from my classmates. In her lexicon, being attractive necessitated fair skin, and again, I thwarted her by insisting on playing sports outdoors, flaunting tan lines and flatly refusing any of her remedial concoctions. We agreed on little.

But now and again, when the fancy struck her, she took to the kitchen to produce her one masterpiece: a perfectly creamy, delicately sweetened phirni, fragrant with cardamom and a whisper of saffron. I was powerless to resist it. During those interludes, all hostilities ceased. I ate with abandon and relish, I let her smooth my hair and patiently listened each time to the accompanying story on the process of this miracle dessert—how the milk had to be stirred constantly, the rice had to be ground fine but not too fine and how she'd spent hours perfecting it. All of it—her voice, the taste of the phirni, cool in the small glass dishes in which it was set and that velvety, spiced scent—was deeply comforting.

Now, even years later, that combination of smells still leads to a powerful rush of emotion. I suppose it could be filed neatly under the Madeleine Effect. In fact, what Proust suggests, in *A la Recherche du Temps Perdu* published over a century ago, about the potency of olfactory memory is quite true. Once an odour is experienced, the context in which it occured and the emotional value of that experience fuses. This odour-associative learning[55] is that flood of whispers in your head that a single fragrance can unleash; the power to carry you away to a different time and place.

Science has known for a while that, for all practical purposes,[56] smell and taste are the same, and most of what we think of as taste is really just smell, the tongue being sadly limited in what it can discern compared to the nose. When I taste saffron, what I am really experiencing are the major constituent molecules: safranal, which gives it that

55. Trygg Engen, *The Perception of Odors*, Academic Press, Massachusetts, 1982.

56. Rachel Herz, *The Scent of Desire: Discovering Our Enigmatic Sense of Smell*, HarperCollins, New York, 2007, p. 197: Herz explains this succinctly: '... flavour is the combination of the basic taste sensations with smell ... Our brains trick us by seamlessly knitting together the sensations of taste and smell to give us the flavours that make up our food world.'

characteristic aroma and the picrocrocin, which is responsible for the slightly bitter taste. A third aspect, crocin, is what gives saffron its dark, earthy red colour, so restful to the eye.

Where flowers are picked, processing usually awaits, and I followed the crocus blooms to this next stage, which takes place, not in a factory or similar industrial area but rather more intimately, in the grower's own home—also home to Bharat Saffron, his brand.

It was a traditional Kashmiri home: wooden, with window frames painted the blue of a clear sky, a small driveway with a border of flowers. Downstairs were the family living quarters, and upstairs, where we went, was a mid-sized room. It was bare, save for the carpeted floor covered by plain white cotton sheets on which six men sat in a circle, mounds of saffron between them, and the air thick with its warm, spiced aroma.

The context of each rare and perfumed botanical, its origin and provenance is what completes its story. Saffron, inseparable as it is from Kashmir, seemed perfectly represented by the scene in that room: the sheets stained red-gold, the pherans and low hum of kishtwari and the warming cup of kehwa offered to me, also flavoured with saffron. It made absolute sense.

An important factor at this stage of the harvest is how the saffron threads are removed, or how much of the style tissue is left on the coloured clavate branches: less is naturally better. The thread removal and drying is exacting and tiring work—a single gram of saffron requires approximately 200 flowers to be processed. As I watched the men work, it became clearer why saffron is known to be the most labour-intensive spice. Everything is done manually. The delicate threads are removed and then dried using sieves. This sieving and the gentle breaking apart of the threads by hand is done repeatedly, patiently until the texture is silken. The men were doing all of this effortlessly it seemed, all the while softly talking to one another, their fingers moving almost independently as they worked through the small piles of velveteen red-gold filaments.

At first, my presence felt like an intrusion; I was the lone woman in a room full of men. My silent observation too seemed to cause some discomfiture, though everyone was unfailingly polite. However, after thirty minutes, when all I continued to do was scribble notes and sip my tea, they slowly became more at ease. I was no longer a threat. Now, I was invited to take a closer look at the process, to touch the saffron and feel its luxuriant texture, admire its beautiful hue which mirrors that of the chinars outside. One of the men, Aatir Masudi, told me he has been doing this work for eight years. Showing me his fingertips, stained semi-permanently with orange, he said that the work is like second nature now. 'When I first started, it was difficult, now it is just like a habit,' he laughed. And well it might be, since it is what he does all year, from 9 a.m. to 5 p.m., processing approximately 250 grams of saffron in seven hours.

As a result of all of this hard work, Bharat Saffron's product, Rakib told me, is of the finest grade and retails for Rs 250 a gram. These are sold in tiny, clear plastic boxes. I watched as he carried out a small demonstration of the packaging, another process that takes place in the same room. He pulled out a mid-sized metal box, very much like the kind you'd expect to hold secret treasure (and, therefore, completely appropriate) that contained about 1.5 kilograms of saffron, a small pair of scales and a set of plastic containers. Opening the box, he lifted some of the saffron onto the palm of his hand to show me its quality: the even thickness of the strands, their rich colour. He then weighed and then packed it into the clear box, which he sealed with a sticker.

Since practically every brand claims unimpeachable purity when it comes to saffron, I recognised Rakib's proclamation of his product's credentials woven into this show-and-tell of the process.

The world over, as much in history as it is today, adulteration of saffron has been rampant, with Pliny the Elder lamenting circa 77 CE that 'there is nothing so much adulterated as saffron'.[57]

Adulterants are used to increase weight and improve colour, thus reducing the price or increasing the profits. Tests have found substances from the expected—turmeric powder or other parts of the saffron flower—to the less expected: borax, glycerine and even plant fibres used for brooms. A two-year-old study conducted in India found that half of all saffron sold in the nation is adulterated, and none of the samples examined met the requirements for classification as Grade 1—not even those from Kashmir, which is further proof that cultivation in the state needs some re-examination.

---

57. Pliny the Elder (Ed. by John Bostock, M.D., F.R.S., H.T. Riley, Esq., B.A.), *The Natural History*, Vol. 21, Ch. 17, available at: http://data.perseus.org/citations/urn:cts:latinLit:phi0978.phi001.perseus-eng1:21.17.

Notes taken, tea drunk and thanks given, I was ready to leave the cocoon of the room and proceed to the Pampore market where Bharat Saffron and other Kashmiri brands sold their product. It was also where saffron oil would be available as well, although distillation, I was told, is not done in Kashmir where the spice is directly consumed. I reached the car, only to be informed that, during the time I had been inside, things had changed. An 'encounter' had taken place in nearby Pulwama. A local man, a supposed militant, had been shot somewhere along the road we had taken to get to Pampore, and it was best if we abandoned further plans and returned instead to Srinagar, this time via the main highway.

I was already plotting a return the next day, or the one after, whenever an all-clear was sounded. But Kashmir is nothing if not unpredictable. The evening brought rain along with a steep drop in temperature and leaden clouds that didn't look like they were merely transiting. For the next thirty-six hours, it rained. A harsh wind blew, howling and felling trees, then abated, but the rain carried on steadily. On the third day, the rain turned to fat, white flakes. The first snow of the year, weeks too early, spell-binding nonetheless. It brought a hush. The air turned crystalline: cold, clear and cutting. To my Delhi-dwelling lungs, poached in smog, the quality of that air was a sharp shock—it almost hurt. Once again, I thought once more of my grandmother who, on holidays in Shimla, would insist that my cousins and I, aged variously between four and ten, go on walks and 'do deep breathing'. At that point, the directive had baffled me—I thought I was breathing just fine—but now, it made perfect sense.

I spent a week in Srinagar, waking each morning ready to return to Pampore, and being thwarted by the weather that was putting on a dramatic show: searing wind, snow and freezing sleet. The snow transformed the landscape completely. I'd arrived in time to catch the last of the autumn sunrays filtered through the rich foliage. Nothing was recognisable now, blanketed as the landscape was in dazzling snow, trees bare and stark against the endless white below and grey above. The silence was enormous.

The days I spent waiting, writing, watching the snow, playing in it with the guest house owner's lively cocker spaniel, fretting over the news of cancelled flights were punctuated by constant cups of warming kehwa, so much better suited to the weather and to contemplation than standard milk tea or coffee. The accompanying fragrance of saffron kept me company in the absence of any chance to revisit Pampore's fields or market.

I bought a packet of the tea and brought it back home in an attempt to keep the memory of my trip alive. Later, back in a laboratory, I discovered another obstacle—no saffron oil.

Because of the spice's inherent antibacterial and anti-fungal properties, steam-distilled saffron oil finds use in food preservation and in ayurvedic prescriptions,[58] but has mostly

58. Naveen Patnaik, *The Garden of Life: An Introduction to The Healing Plants of India*, Aquarian/HarperCollins, Delhi, 1993, p. 143: 'Ayurveda uses small quantities of saffron in mixtures that are drunk to tone the uterus after childbirth and to regulate gynecological disorders, as well as for fevers, spasmodic coughs, and asthma. Saffron is also thought to be effective in improving vision and for curing melancholia.'

fallen out of favour in fragrance labs because of its scarcity and expense. Predictably, to see the making of a real itr zafraan I needed to return to Kannauj, still the repository for every traditional perfume formula and method. A considerable amount of time had passed since last I had been. The approach to town now boasted a freshly metalled road, a flyover and a certain new affluence that showed in the row of air-conditioned shops selling home appliances. The old centre, however, had retained its medieval feel.

Within those narrow lanes, I made my way to ML Ramnarain Perfumers, a family-run distillery and business that attempts to find a balance between the past and the present. Pranjal Kapoor, who helms the business, feels strongly about the need to introduce traditional itr and ruh to perfumers internationally as ingredients that could potentially find their way into fine fragrances. They supply oils, primarily cypriol (nagarmotha), or *Cyperous scariosus*, to the Swiss fragrance creation house, Firminich. Nagarmotha grows wild in central India, and its oil, which smells herbal, with damp mushroom notes, is distilled from its roots, like vetiver. India is a primary producer of this ingredient, which sells for Rs 20,000 a kilogram. The business also supplies valerian oil (which, when undiluted, smells powerfully overripe, not unlike unwashed synthetic socks), and trade in a few others, like carrot-seed oil, jatamansi, ginger and black pepper oils, a large percentage of which are exported.

Since the bulk of the business is focused on trade in these oils, Kapoor said it leaves him with little time (but enough creative drive) to produce more niche itrs like mitti, shamama and, of course, saffron, which he does only on order for buyers who have the appreciation (and deep pockets—saffron itr sells for over Rs 2 lakh a kilogram) for rare, beautiful ingredients.

The process, after all, was far from a simple one. It began with Kashmiri saffron being weighed carefully on a set of balance scales: 100 grams of the red-gold strands on one side, tiny hexagonal bronze weights on the other. Once Jawahar, an old deft hand in charge of the process, was satisfied, he took it to a corner of an airy room that is part-office, part-museum dedicated to a more graceful era. Here, he had a steel bucket full of saffron hydrosol (the water left over from a previous distillation) from which he used a few ladlefuls, enough to moisten the saffron well. When he was satisfied, Jawahar took handfuls of the mixture to a well-used grinding stone—a sil batta—and ground the mixture to a rough paste. Squatting on his haunches, he worked in silence, absorbed and meticulous. All around, the air was thick with the hay-and-honey notes of the spice he was grinding. It usually takes him close to thirty minutes of grinding, a vital first step. As Kapoor explained, 'The strands have to open up so that the oils and active molecules are released.'

To see the next step, we walked to the distillery via a perpendicular lane, along the side of which lay an open drain that sometimes ran with rose and saffron water, adding a sweetness to the air as the scents asserted themselves over the smell of cowpats. It was a mere few dozen metres away, but twice we were forced to turn back because of a local hazard—a bull with an unpredictable temper that liked to roam the area and, on occasion, casually terrorise pedestrians.

The distillery, when we finally reached it, resembled all the others I had seen, with its rows of degs on earthern, wood-fired stoves and a smoky, fragrant atmosphere. I watched Jawahar tie the ground saffron into small bundles of plain cotton cloth, which then went into a copper pot along with a few kilograms of hydrosol ('Everything is measured in kilograms here, there is no smaller amount,' said Kapoor) to prevent scalding the saffron. The bhapka, or receiver, already had sandalwood oil in it. The method preferred by Kapoor is to distill a small amount multiple times over. So, 100 grams of saffron in three kilograms of hydrosol is distilled thrice over in a small pot. This batch was currently on day two.

Each distillation lasts four days, and the saffron is replenished on the fifth. 'The process happens in three stages, which means that about fifteen days go into the making,' said Kapoor. At the end of the fortnight, he will have one kilogram of pure itr to be kept aside for the person who has specially ordered it. And indeed, it is near impossible to find a pure itr zafraan at a retail outlet: 'I would say that 99 per cent of the stuff you find for retail has safranal in it,' he grunted, shaking his head.

The final stage is the 'water bath', a uniquely Kannaujian finishing touch. Instead of a bhapka, the saffron in its potli gets immersed in a distillate of saffron and sandalwood oil collected from the previous stage and gently heated, a kind of poaching that really infuses the sandalwood with every bit of saffron possible.

Finally, the resulting oil is to be given a two-day rest to settle and gather itself, before being decanted and placed into separating funnels to split the oil and water, which is never as easy as it sounds. 'Sometimes, separating the oil gets tricky,' Kapoor explained. 'Sometimes, we need to use rock salt to change the density of the water, so that the oil becomes more evident and easier to extract.'

Back in the office, I smelt a few samples from previous distillations, one of which was a zafraani gulab, made by distilling saffron over an itr gulab (also made with sandalwood). It smelt like pure velvet: plush, floral, warm and rich. Another was an itr zafraan, one that had a few months to mature. This too was beautifully smooth, the sandalwood and saffron having come together perfectly with no hard edges at all. The only caveat is that they have a limited shelf life, of a year at most before the itr can sometimes begin to smell slightly off. Many factors can influence this—the quality of the sandalwood oil used, how well the distillation is done and if there is any water left unseparated in the formula.

'Frankly, the beauty of the process lies in the post-distillation treatment of an itr,' Kapoor told me, tapping the glass bottle lightly. 'The art, skill and experience lies in how you extract the oil, how well you separate it.'

Carelessness during the process, not enough supervision, storing an itr in a damp place—such factors can spell doom for a product this delicate, and a lack of quality control is, in great part why, as Kapoor put it, 'Kannauj is badnaam', its reputation suffering from being associated with pervasive adulteration.

He told me that it is precisely to counter this impression that ML Ramnarain Perfumers rigorously tests the quality of its oils and itrs on a gas-liquid chromatograph machine. They are also tested for refractive index, specific gravity and optical rotation, all of which are important, particularly in the case of oils being exported, since any discrepancies usually result in entire shipments being returned and, consequently, considerable losses.

The rules for export to Europe are highly stringent, especially when compared to the Middle East, which has long been an established market for Indian essential oils and fragrances. A major difference between the two territories is that the use of DOP, so common in Kannauj, is not permitted in Europe. In practical terms, this does not only mean that it cannot be part of the preparation of an itr but also that the entire vicinity where the distillation process occurs needs to be free of the chemical, right down to the plastic sacks used for the transport of flowers and herbs.

'If a small fibre from one of the bags accidentally makes its way into a distillation, it will show up in the analysis because the bags are PET, and the peak [of the analysis graph] looks similar to DOP,' said Kapoor.

Even in a playing field where natural, luxurious ingredients are labouriously grown, harvested and distilled with such care, the effort and expense that saffron demands seems daunting. Most perfumers rely on synthetic molecules when they need to add any of saffron's facets to a fragrance. In the laboratory, I pulled some of these bottles off the shelves and explored them, wafting blotters dipped deftly in the liquids before my nose, inhaling with solemn concentration to tease out the facets. Safranal, of course, is the organic compound isolated from the spice; it smells spicy, floral and mildly medicinal. There's *Safraliene* developed by fragrance manufacturer Givaudan, which has the distinct saffron aroma, but plays up its complex, leathery tones, and then there's beta-cyclocitral, similar but a bit more herbal and fruity. There is an entire world of nuance and abstraction among the synthetics, right there in the thousands of amber glass bottles lining the shelves in the laboratory; they offer efficiency, precision and cost-effectiveness.

And yet, having smelt, seen and followed the making of saffron oil all the way through, it is equally true that the beauty of such a fragrance isn't just in its component parts and molecules but in the whole. The relationship it has with the land, the people who cultivate and harvest it—that is ultimately what makes it complex, complete and nigh impossible to replace.

Oud

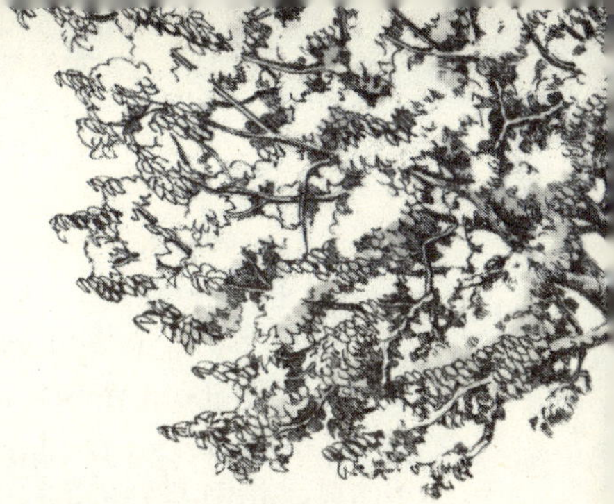

LIKE SMELLS, THERE are certain other features of a home that remain ingrained in memory long after the house itself is gone. One such image that comes to mind is that of an upright piano standing sentinel in a corner of the dining room of the Public Works Department flat we lived in, the witness to decades' worth of meals, conversations and games of make-believe in which it often starred as a central prop. It served its primary purpose as a musical instrument as well, of course, just not at my hands. My sister began learning to play early in her life, and as she progressed through grades and books of complicated-looking sheet music, I listened to the tunes, sang along with a few, poked fun at her mistakes, but never really considered learning myself. We had our roles; she played music, I played sports.

Some ideas percolate slowly though, I suppose. Perhaps having had Mozart and Strauss as regular background music to my mundane adolescent and childhood doings left an impression after all, because later (much, much later) in my life, I decided I wanted to learn the piano, and to play classical music at that. The upright piano was still around, now in a corner of my father's dining room, unused and out of tune, and I was going through a phase in which both curiosity and nostalgia figured prominently. I wanted to learn, to study once again, this time not with a view to gainful employment as had been the case in my twenties but as an indulgence. To immerse myself in subjects I loved, perhaps even learn something about myself along the way. It wasn't quite yet a mid-life issue, but the Jungian theory about it fit rather well. Jung posits that the first half of life is given over to succeeding socially and achieving an 'entrenchment in the outer world', but what comes after that's done demands a significance of its own—something dictated by the aspects of our selves that lie latent and have been experienced very little, or not at all. To wit, music. And perfumery.

I found a music teacher, moved the piano to my own dining room, where it could be restored to its original purpose, bought the necessary books and began learning a little every day—tentative and slow, as I had been when I first began smelling. My teacher, a hard-smoking Russian woman with a flair for the theatrical and the morose, started me off gently: beginners' theory, scales, short etudes. This is fine, I thought to myself, not too bad at all. Like smelling roses, jasmine and velvety, caramel-tinged balsams. It was relatively easy-going, until it wasn't. There was an increasing number of layers to grapple with: reading the notes, figuring out where they fell, playing both legato and staccato and maintaining tempo. I did my best but still hit a wall at the simplest baroque compositions. Something about the polyphonic texture, the contrapuntal notes required my brain to bend in ways it couldn't seem to. Somewhere between my mind and my hands was a wide rift, and I kept stumbling into it. It was, in fact, a lot like my first olfactory encounter with oud.

In perfumery, oud has been the trend that refuses to leave, around the world. I'd heard of it before I smelt it (or so I thought) in expensive perfumes that were rich with woods and musks and marketed themselves as 'oriental', the imagery alluding to the Western idea of a sensual East. Indeed, perfumery continues to be an area of the arts to which Edward Said's critique of Orientalism from 1978[59]

---

59. Edward Said, *Orientalism*, Routledge & Kegan Paul, London, 1978, p. 12: This one paragraph from the introduction to the text puts forth the idea later explored in greater depth, that of the West slowly defining and taking ownership of the East: 'Therefore, Orientalism is not a mere political subject matter or field that is reflected passively by culture, scholarship, or institutions; nor is it a large and diffuse collection of texts about the Orient; nor is it representative and expressive of some nefarious "Western" imperialist plot to hold down the "Oriental" world. It is rather a distribution of geopolitical awareness into aesthetic, scholarly, economic, sociological, historical, and philological texts; it is an elaboration not only of a basic geographical distinction (the world is made up of two unequal halves, Orient and Occident) but also of a whole series of "interests" which, by such means as scholarly discovery, philological reconstruction, psychological analysis, landscape and sociological description, it not only creates but also maintains; it is, rather than expresses, a certain will or intention to understand, in some cases to control, manipulate, even to incorporate, what is a manifestly different (or alternative and novel) world; it is, above all, a discourse that is by no means in direct, corresponding relationship with political power in the raw, but rather is produced and exists in an uneven exchange with various kinds of power, shaped to a degree by the exchange with power political (as with a colonial or imperial establishment), power intellectual (as with reigning sciences like comparative linguistics or anatomy, or any of the modern policy sciences), power cultural (as with orthodoxies and canons of taste, texts, values), power moral (as with ideas about what "we" do and what "they" cannot do or understand as "we" do). Indeed, my real argument is that Orientalism is-and does not simply represent-a considerable dimension of modern political-intellectual culture, and as such has less to do with the Orient than it does with "our" world.'

remains wholly applicable. So, it isn't surprising to me that a material so closely bound up with India made its way back into the mainstream via a discovery on far shores.

Voluptuous as these perfumes were, nothing prepared me for the first smell of the real thing. I encountered it at a traditional itr store in Old Delhi, in the innards of Chandni Chowk, virtually in the shadow of the walled city where, I imagine, its fragrance once wafted down halls. I sat in a small store with an experienced perfumer where, at her request, the proprietor pulled out samples of the different grades of oud he had. As I leaned over to sniff a strip that had been dipped in a bronze-coloured oil, eyes half-closed, I was as expectant as a lover. In the next instant, my eyes snapped open in surprise. The first note, and the most insistent, was a cheesy, Gorgonzola one. No smooth, incensed woods, but something darker and almost feral came off the strip. As I smelt different ouds, I encountered more faces of it: some sweeter and almost floral, and some that balanced on the edge of beautiful and putrid. Much like the sheet music I struggled to read and play as instructed, all of them demanded something of me—attention, study and effort. They weren't going to offer up their secrets to the undedicated.

So, I took my time and returned to oud again and again, each time learning a little more and getting closer to deciphering just why this particular fragrance had made so firm a mark on the Indian, and universal, smellscape.

As far back as the first century BCE, agarwood (or aloeswood, as it is alternately referred to in historical texts) finds mention in the *Arthashastra*. It is written of as a luxury material that is as rarefied, if not more than sandalwood, and essential to any prosperous king's treasury. It had already by then established itself in collective imagination as important and beautiful.[60]

There are passages in the Mahabharata that describe in detail the tribute paid to the five Pandava brothers from kingdoms across the land eager to form or cement alliances. These deal with the description of the rajasuya sacrificial rites the Pandava brothers performed before the fateful game of dice in which Yudhisthira loses all. The event is attended by rulers of kingdoms across the land, all of whom bring tributes, notable among which are those offered by kingdoms[61] from the northeast of what is now India, a region known even then to be rich in aloeswood, which fittingly formed the bulk of the tribute made by them. Similarly, in the *Harsacharita*

60. James McHugh, *Sandalwood and Carrion: Smell in Indian Religion and Culture*, New York: Oxford University Press, 2012, p. 159: 'The most important aromatics in medieval South Asia were both exotic and expensive, not unlike spices in medieval Europe. Perfumes made of such exotica, as well as gemstones and other luxury commodities were closely associated with the ideal lifestyle of the king and the cultivated man-bout-town.'

61. Ibid., p. 169: Mahabharata 2.48.8-11 (as quoted in): 'In the epic, they are noted by a resentful Duryodhana who later recounts them to his father, saying, 'Those kings who are on the other side of the Himalaya, or the mountain behind which the sun rises, and who are the edge of the ocean of *Varisena* on both sides of the Lohitya river. And those kiratas who eat fruits and roots, who have clothes of skins, brought loads of sandalwood and aloeswood, and of *kaliyaka*, as well as heaps of skins, jewels, gold, and perfumes.'

(606–649 BC), a work concerning the rule of King Harsha in Kannauj,[62] there is mention of gifts brought by an envoy from a kingdom in the northeast. Several of these are aromatic in nature: cooling camphor, musk pods, cubebs, nutmeg and, most thrillingly, entire silken sackfuls of rare aloeswood, along with bamboo tubes full of its rich oil. King Harsha was apparently so amazed by these gifts he felt that he was left with little choice but to accept the proffered alliance and seal the deal by offering, in return, fragrant sandalwood paste.

Spice and fragrance, while not as conspicuous as horses, palaces, jewellery or other markings of a wealthy life, were still important status symbols—objects of desire that conferred distinction upon the user.

This remains as true today as it was then. Objects of desire (and often of no practical value) continue to provide social mileage, with merely the nature of the object changing from one age to the next. Fashions move and change, and often come full circle, as seems to be the case with oud. Though there has never really been a time in which it wasn't considered precious, it was, for a long while, overshadowed by modern perfumery's many other materials and developments. Then, perhaps around a decade ago, it made a comeback, most notably with *Oud Wood* by Tom Ford. Since then, it has found its way into perfumes across brands, in compositions that pair it with classic foils like rose and amber, or even pit it against contrasting ones like citruses. There's practically no new ground left to break.

62. Ibid., p. 170.

For a connoisseur, though, or for the truly curious, getting closer to the heart of the material involves taking a path less modern, one that leads back to oils and blends that are closer to the original ways that agarwood was used, and that now have begun to feel new again.

Following just such a path, I made my way to Mumbai where, in a spare apartment above a busy supermarket in Chembur, I met Zakir Hussein Laskar, owner of a niche Indian fragrance brand called Ahom Oud. I had been following it on social media with interest for its compositions that remain true to a traditional style of perfumery. He uses a very Indian palette of all-natural ingredients, and uses them in hefty, unstinting doses. Some of his blends—like the classic shamama that has no exact formula and changes with every perfumer—use a maceration of real ambergris in sandalwood oil. His soliflore itrs, like jasmine and rose, are made as they were always intended—distilled over pure sandalwood oil and not the chemical alternatives that the oil has long been replaced with.

Far more interesting, though, and the reason I'd sought him out, are his perfumes and itrs that showcase the finest Indian oud, an ingredient that he knows and understands intimately, and that his family have traded in for three generations before him. His father, he tells me, was well known in the industry and had been inducted into the agarwood business at just thirteen years of age. He was a part of teams that explored the forests of Assam looking for the trees. These teams would have been granted a 'mahal', a permission that allowed individuals to sell forest produce they found within a defined portion of hilly forest for a certain time period. The rules applied to all areas that came under the original Assam Forest Regulations of 1891 which, at the time, included all of Arunachal Pradesh. The broad term 'timber' used in the rules included all sorts of wood, but arguably the most valuable trees were the *Aquilaria malaccensis*: evergreen agarwood trees. To save time, the harvested wood would be distilled at a camp set up at the base of the hill. An interesting and little-known fact that I learnt was that this part of the process was largely overseen by the women in the family, who manned the copper sills constantly, while the men came and went. Many of them developed finely honed noses this way, and Zakir counts his mother among them: 'I always ask her opinion on any new oils. Even if she is in the middle of cooking a fermented fish curry, she can still smell an oud and is able to tell the quality and identify the notes.'

Phytogeographically speaking, the *Aquillaria* species is found mainly in the northeast of India, and across the borders in Myammar and Bhutan, in China and the Indo-Malaysian archipelago all the way to Papua New Guinea. What makes the tree so valuable, and what 'aloeswood' or 'agarwood' really refers to, is the resin that it may contain—a result of the tree's natural reaction to an infection. If a tree is infected with a certain parasitic mould, it protects itself by producing a resin high in volatile oils to curb the fungus. The resin itself can be scraped or cut away and burnt for its fragrance as aloeswood historically was, but not distilled. It is the wood of that particular tree which is distilled. The higher the quality of the resin on the tree, the better the oil in the wood—and the oil thus produced is rich, and far more nuanced than I knew, as I discovered on that warm, early summer afternoon.

As we sat there, Zakir pulled out vials of ouds from a painted wooden box, and handed me tiny amounts on smelling strips, telling me the name and provenance of each. Much as with fine wine, terroir and year matter for these oils. Though Assam (or Hindi Oud, as it is often called) is an umbrella term for oud from the northeast of India, regional differences in soil and microclimate contribute to each fragrance, making it distinct.

The first one I smelt was from Manipur, harvested in 2006. It was smoky, with a sweet pipe tobacco note that took me right back to the 1980s, to a brief period when my father switched from smoking cigarettes to pipes. I used to like playing with pipe cleaners and hung about when he lit up so I could sniff the smouldering tobacco leaves.

Next up was a wood chip, a pinky fingernail's worth of *Aquilaria crassna* from Thailand, nestled next to a bit of smouldering coal. The smoke it gave off smelt spicy, rich and animalic. Refined, but just a bit wild as well. Such a tiny bit of wood could burn for twenty minutes, creating a near-hypnotic atmosphere around it, justifying its coveted status and price tag. The next bit of resin I tried was from a twenty-year-old Assamese harvest, which burnt with a more conservative woody note, with a hint of hay-like sweetness. In musical terms, if the previous was a symphony, this one was a simple etude—a beginner's agarwood. It was, I imagine, the smoke that had scented the halls, rooms and darbars of emperors all through Indian history. The Mughal emperors, and Akbar in particular, had leant towards this practice. In the section that deals with the emperor's khushbu khana, the *Ain-i-Akbari* mentions not only that his royal majesty had himself ceremoniously weighed against perfumes (as also gold and silver) on special occasions but also that he liked his chambers liberally scented with aloeswood smoke.

Returning to the oils before me, I smelt a 1999 harvest from Laos that Zakir said 'has the profile closest to the famous Hainan wood from China'. This close relative of that prized oud had a subtle sweetness to it, unusual in an oud. It had, to my mind, aged like fine wine in a temperature-controlled cellar. A 2018 harvest from upper Assam called Panbari Reserve came close to the oud I had first encountered: dark wood and ripe cheese; robust and assertive. Another, from Thailand again, smelt of overripe tropical fruits, with a distinctive bitterness owing to the fact that it had been distilled from the tree's root, not the stem. The last one and my definite favourite was a beautifully refreshing—not a term I'd ever have associated with this oil—oud from Mizoram. A 1994 harvest, named 'Lushai' after the tribe from the area, it smelt of grass, moss and the forests it came from, and had an almost vetiver-like greenness to it that made for a very pleasant change from the baroque notes of the others.

Classical, romantic, lilting—so much more than I knew or expected. Almost all of them Indian, and all those from one slice of the country, namely the northeastern states, but especially Assam where the trees were a native species, requiring no coaxing at all to flourish. So, there I flew to next, landing in Jorhat on a mild, sunny afternoon perfectly placed between Assam's ferocious monsoon and frosty winter, and found the city a pleasant surprise. Knowing it to be the administrative centre for upper Assam, I'd expected the sprawl and disorganisation that characterise so many smaller Indian cities, and while there was some of that, it was limited to the town centre, which featured the usual jumble of rutted roads, a mix of shops and haphazard traffic. Veering off the main road, I was greeted by narrow streets that suddenly fell quiet and were clean. They were bordered by orderly homes fronted with gardens and vegetable patches ringed with neat bamboo fences. Goats and chickens walked serenely by. It seemed peaceful, almost bucolic.

Though standard three- and four-star hotels did exist in the city centre, I had decided to eschew the forgettable comfort of those and to spend the limited time I had staying on a family-run tea estate and guest house instead. Set on over 500 acres, it had tea shrubs, fruit trees and a fishing pond, and genteel single-storeyed bungalows speckled here and there. The whole place radiated a sense of sanctuary.

Tea estates in Assam are quite commonly dotted with agarwood trees, but this estate was an exception, and so my first encounter with the *Aquilaria* trees was twenty kilometres away in Titabor. That was where I went to meet Bikash Baruah, the general secretary of the All Sanchi Growers Association of Assam (ASGAA)—'sanchi' being the local term for agar. He was a grower himself, as well as a small-scale distiller, and as I had smelt some of the oils supplied by him to Zakir when I was in Mumbai, I was eager to see his process and unit first-hand.

Over tea and an endless array of snacks that his wife generously served, Baruah told me about how for him, as for most in the region, the familiarity with agar began in childhood and ran generations deep.

'Every household here grows the trees and knows about them,' he said, sipping from his cup. 'When I was in school, my friends and I would talk about which of our families had sold a tree and what we had gotten from the earnings. Someone would have a new shirt, toy or a bike. I knew it was important but I didn't know more than that, and I did not know the true value of these trees.'

While that is now a distant memory for him, not very much has changed in the region. The agar trade in upper Assam is still a somewhat small-scale and family-run one. Every household has at least a few trees in their yards, often growing alongside other cash crops like tea or areca nut, and they are treated as a kind of insurance scheme or safety net. Selling agar trees can see a family through lean times or happy ones, like a child's wedding, higher education or health emergencies, as was the case with a neighbour Baruah told me about, one who required urgent medical treatment and sold a tree to raise the cash. Useful as this is, the downside of the practice is that farmers rarely get an amount that reflects the real worth of agarwood. Young trees sold in haste, around half a decade old, fetch only some Rs 5,000–10,000. Technically, a tree is considered mature at fifteen years, after which the price of the wood only keeps rising. Needless to say, traders attempt to get the best deals they can, and status quo holds. Rather more significantly, farmers at present aren't

able to do more than harvest their trees and sell wood to such middlemen, thanks to a set of labyrinthine (and mostly outdated) official rules.

In India, *Aquilaria* trees are a protected species under the 1972 Wildlife Protection Act, and trade in the wood is regulated under the Convention on International Trade in Endangered Species of Wild Fauna and Flora (CITES) to which India is a signatory. CITES prohibits the harvest of 'wild' wood, which is what agarwood is classified as. Export, except for re-export—goods coming from another country and going back there—is barred, since a new policy that takes into account the fact that 90 per cent of agarwood in India is now plantation-grown hasn't yet been formulated. Wild trees were abundant a few decades ago. The area we're in—previously the undivided Sibsagar district—parcelled into smaller districts in the 1980s was originally forested land that, over time, has been cultivated and built upon. Some wild trees do still exist in protected areas, but for the most part, they have been poached and illegally traded out of existence, much like sandalwood has in the southern states. As things stand, more trees are grown in plantations sustainably, but international trade is still barred, and a new policy would need to address this.

'My first objective in creating ASGAA was to safeguard farmers' interests, but I also gradually noticed that the government barely has any knowledge on this subject. Every time I filed an RTI, they had no answers or information; it is like an unregulated industry,' Baruah said.

Behind his house, 3,000 *Aquilaria* trees are spread

over four bighas, or 1.3 acres of land, many of which have propagated effortlessly from the original saplings that were planted by his father, having the remarkable ability to grow even in water or soil contaminated by heavy industry by-products, conditions that other crops would refuse to survive in. We walked through the wooded land among the slim, graceful trees with their pale grey bars and evergreen canopies, some as old as eighty years, to the edge of the property where a river, locally called the Kashajan, ran. It was just a rivulet now, dark and slow, but Baruah told me that in the monsoon it showed a different face, a rushing mass of water that the children were warned to stay well away from.

I was reminded again of the India-as-the-Garden of Eden theory.[63] Indian rivers, in the marvel-strewn, mythical East, were said to have flowed with gems, rare spices and, of course, aloeswood. All one needed to do was fish it out.

As we walked, Baruah pointed out trees that were infected, their pale trunks marked with dark, coin-sized holes where the borer insects had got to them. While an infestation of this kind would be cause for alarm, if not outright panic, in any other crop, here it was nothing short of a brilliant stroke of luck. An infected *Aquilaria* tree is the only kind with commercial value, the only kind that produces agarwood. Though naturally infected trees are a rarity, the phenomenon seemed to be fairly common here, another fact that marks Assamese agarwood as exceptional.

---

63. Paul Freedman, *Out of The East: Spices and the Medieval Imagination*, Yale University Press, New Haven, 2008, p. 94–5.

The *Zeuzera conferta* Walker is the pest responsible for this good fortune. Known in Assamese as pukh (simply 'insect'), the wood borer is common in Southeast Asia, Sri Lanka, Bangladesh, the Andaman Islands and is particularly prevalent in Northeast India. The larvae of this borer infest the tree's trunk and allow for the microbial infection to develop, which then sets off the complex interaction between insect, plant and various microscopic arcana that allows for the formation of fragrant resin. As the larvae feed their way up the tree, spreading the infection, the wood begins to form dark streaks that turn a darker shade and finally black, marbling the previously healthy tree. Ironically, as the tree decays—the canopy withering, the trunks canker-riddled—its worth increases. The agarwood that forms is, in a way, a swan song.

This isn't luck that is guaranteed to last, however. Aside from the issue of how arbitrarily selective the insects are in deciding which tree they will attack, these borers themselves are now dying out, and their preservation, as well as an all-natural way of obtaining agarwood, is another of ASGAA's aims.

'Only from November to March, when it is not the plucking period for tea, is pesticide not sprayed, and the borers take shelter in the *Aquilaria* trees,' explained Baruah. 'The pesticide is not good for them. Somehow, they are still surviving, but soon they will suffer ill health.'

Dark portents indeed. The alternate, already widely in use, is artificial infection, where the trees are injected with fungal isolates, the solution drilled in or administered via bottle as you would a saline drip to a dehydrated patient. The results are more dependable and consistent, even though the quality of agarwood and oud so obtained isn't in the same league as that from naturally infected trees.

His own trees, however, are a veritable treasure and meant to be preserved, said Baruah. He has decided not to sell them. 'I am going to keep these for research purposes, as it has become too rare to find old growth *Aquilaria malaccensis* trees,' he said.

There are stories, though, about old *Aquilaria* trees still growing in remote regions of Nagaland or other hilly northeastern states, of tribal men who occasionally cut them and bring pieces of wood down and sell them for a pittance because they don't really know that those ordinary-looking bits of blackened wood are practically priceless. Stories also of agents from Hojai with deep pockets and informers everywhere. Men who get first dibs on this treasure, secreting it away first to Mumbai, where trade in oud was once bustling, and then onwards, to sell to patrons in the Middle East with even deeper pockets—an entire parallel network that functions like the dark web: nefarious, almost certainly illegal and resistant to deep investigation.

Dusk had fallen while we were among the trees and darkness would follow swiftly, though it wasn't yet 5 p.m. (by all rights, the northeast should have its own time zone as it is an hour ahead of Indian Standard Time). I left, with plans to return the following day in order to see the distillation unit housed in the bamboo-and-cane outhouse. The unit had been running for almost a week already, and emanated that signature woody fragrance when I crossed it.

The next day arrived, just as blue and placid as the previous. In the morning, I appreciatively drank tea picked from the very estate I was leisurely walking around in, accompanied by two of the five dog-residents there. Later, on the drive back to Titabor, more fully awake than I had been the day before, the landscape revealed itself in glorious shades of green, the late October sunlight pouring itself over emerald paddy fields, sprawling tea plantations and banana trees with lush, outsized leaves, showing the countryside at its fertile, peaceful best. I tried to get in as much of it as I could. To come from Delhi with its constant accompaniments of noise, filth and free-floating anxiety, these parts of the country were a revelation and a balm every time I saw them. Here, I could roll down the windows of the car and breathe in a verdant tincture: sap, leaves, soil.

By the time I reached, it was almost noon, and I was graciously invited to join the family meal. Over sumptuous helpings of fish, rice and dal, I asked Baruah how was it that he had diversified into distillation, given that it is not the business he had been engaged in before. His answer was deceptively simple. 'I asked the forest department if I could start a unit and they just told me to go ahead without a permit, as there is no provision in the law for giving one. And I did, because I wanted to get some practical experience, since I get asked many questions on oil and extraction at conferences.'

After the meal, still chewing on a homemade mouth freshener comprising fennel and clove, I was taken to the outhouse and distillation unit at last. Entering it felt like walking into an entire sensory experience. There was the rhythmic sound of wood being chipped as one worker toiled diligently at a chopping block with a serious-looking machete, surrounded by sacks of agarwood. The boilers bubbled away, peacefully lit by shafts of golden light coming in from the cane lattice, sawdust motes dancing in them. It was warm inside with the wood fire burning, and the air was thick with the sensual smell of oud. In a corner was a trough, roughly constructed of concrete and brick, full of wood chips soaking. As Baruah's own trees were not destined for the axe, the wood was bought from neighbours as also from plantations across the northeast and visiting traders who sell the wood left over after the resinous heartwood has been cleaved away. Leftover though it may be, it was still valuable, and I saw how a few pieces were shot through with resin, not enough to make incense-grade chips of, but enough for extraction. At between Rs 400–2,000 per kilogram, this oil, locally called 'boya', is classified not as A Grade, but lower on the scale, making its way into paan masala and zarda, rather than finer scents.

Once the wood has been hacked into chips, it must be soaked for anywhere between one or two months in order for the resin to become more yielding, before it is transferred to the boiler along with water. Of the two boilers running, one had eighty kilograms of chips and sixty litres of water, the other, producing boya, over 100 kilograms of chips.

The process they undergo is a straightforward hydrodistillation, in which the heat generated by the water and steam causes the cell structures of the wood to break down, freeing the essential oils. The steam is carried into a cooling tank to return to liquid form and collected in a vat. The water and oil thus collected, being immiscible, allow for easy separation. Across the world, steam distillation is the method used for extraction of oil from wood, but in Assam, this simpler form is preferred, both for how much easier and cheaper it is, as well as for the quality of oil produced. Zakir swears by the traditional method, insisting that it adds more dimension to the oud: 'Steam-distilled oil is more linear. Think of hydro as a one-pot biryani, cooked on slow dum.'

I was allowed a peep and a sniff of the two vats. The first, of boya, was the colour of butter tinged with green, and smelling correspondingly greener and sourer than the rich, animalic A-Grade oud. It is a not-too-distant cousin, but perhaps a poorer one.

The final step of separating oil and water, usually done with a funnel, is done manually with skilled, deft hands. Oil is skimmed off the surface in quick, sure movements of the palm and collected by wiping on the edge of a steel bowl that resembles, more or less, an oversized soup spoon. As a final step, the oil collected is poured into glass bottles and sunned every afternoon for at least three months, allowing any remaining water to evaporate. And at long last, the entire orchestra of labour, time and attention will have culminated in 100 grams of Assam's finest oud.

Back in Mumbai, I meet Zakir once more, and there is another wooden box opened, revealing another set of bottles bearing his precious compositions.

I smell *Amber Rose* which, apart from its namesake ingredients, also has ambergris alongside oud, and smells lush, warm and syrupy. Next, *Kaafila*, which has sambac jasmine over an almost salty warm oud and khus, which adds earthiness, and finally *Ashraf*, an itr rich with tuberose and sandalwood, musky and velvety with oud. Every composition has come together smoothly, each with the signature stamp of pure Hindi oud, some from the very distillation that I saw, adding heft and velvety warmth. There are no hard edges, nothing of the mistimed notes or clunky pedal work that I continue to try to work through in my own musical endeavours—just the finest symphony.

Vetiver

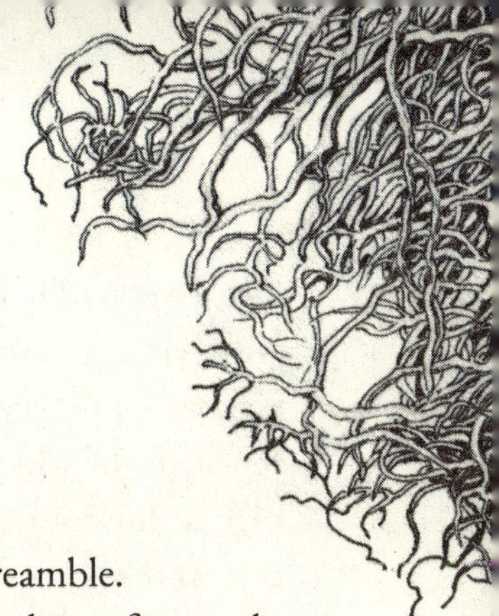

SUMMER IN DELHI arrives with scant preamble. The relief of longer days and endless sunshine after weeks of an enveloping soupy smog in shades of iron and despair gives way fairly quickly to alarm at the temperatures that inch ever upward, and the dramatic dust storms that sweep in from the streets, leaving no household unmarked, no matter how arduously the dusting is carried out. The summer is long, and it is languid—making no move to hurry along or make room for the next season. Brief showers relieve the heat on some days, but it returns in a matter of hours, leaving the city damp and stickily airless. It really isn't for the faint of heart. If you persist though, or if you have no choice but to, you can discover its rhythms and pleasures the way I did as a child in a Delhi that seems impossibly far away now.

My first home in the city, in the Delhi of old, like most at that time, had no air conditioner. Later, one was installed in my parents' bedroom, and on particularly humid nights when a desert cooler was of no help at all, my sister and I were allowed to drag the mattress off our bed onto the floor in their room and sleep there. While this system worked well most of the time, there were the days when working an air conditioner seemed more than the poor, weighed-down electrical grid could endure, and flicking the switch on caused some kind of fault that left us with no electricity at all, just a very still darkness. These nights were spent stoically, with some amount of fretting and liberal lashings of bright yellow, oppressively citronella-scented Odomos mosquito repellent, of which we owned a family-sized tube. On some nights, however, the situation galvanised my father. While my mother chose to resignedly ignore the heat and sweat in silence, he would decide that a visit to the Delhi Electrical Supply Undertaking (DESU, always pronounced as just that one word) premises was in order to lodge a complaint and find out what the problem was. Or, perhaps, he just sought to speed the night along. If my sister and I were awake, we always went along. Those were exciting nights, heading out in the Maruti 800 still in our pyjamas, windows rolled down, arriving at the DESU office. While my father joined the others there with similar grievances, we sat on the edge of the open window, legs inside the car, hands drumming tunes on the roof. Whether any of it led to the electricity being restored, I have no recollection. It seems by now beside the point. The memories of the summers past are what make me look forward to the season each year, and try defiantly to enjoy the dry, shimmering heat, feeling just a bit bereft as it segues into the monsoon, for then I know I must wait another year.

We continued back then to largely rely on the trusted desert cooler to mitigate the heat. It blocked half the window, and the fan kept up a lulling drone as it churned out cool air. In the afternoons, it turned the room dim, a cove that smelt like rush-matting and khus, or vetiver—a pleasing aroma that lingers as much within my recollections as it does more generally around the North Indian summer.

In perfumery around the world, vetiver is lauded for its earthy notes and its ability as a fixative. Various interpretations have resulted in fragrances that bring out its cool, sparkling side or the more languid, moody one. Here in India, however, it has a humbler status, but one that is arguably more beloved for the way in which it finds its way into the daily rhythms of life, and has done for centuries. Sanskrit texts such as the *Amarakosh*,[64] dated to around the sixth century CE, lists aromatics and divides them into sections, such as one concerning herb and forest produce. These were aromatics that were easily available, significant in perfumery, but not in the same league as rare woods and resins. The mark of luxury was conferred only on those scented products that could not be obtained except via long-distance trade and at considerable expense. Such products were exotic and marked out their users as those of superior status. The humble 'usira', as vetiver, was referred to in the ancient Sanskrit texts but never made it onto lists of important aromatics since it was local and inexpensive. Nonetheless, it remained an important part of life's rituals and ayurvedic remedies. Kalidasa, in his play *Shakuntala*,[65] which dates back to about the fourth century CE, makes mention of an ointment of usira, a substance

64. James McHugh, *Sandalwood and Carrion: Smell in Indian Religion and Culture*, Oxford University Press, New York, p. 162.

65. Kalidasa, *Shakuntala or The Lost Ring, An Indian Drama*, Project Gutenberg, April 2004: 'Why, Priyamvada for whose use are you carrying that ointment of usira-root and those lotus leaves with fubres attached to them? What say you? That Sakuntala is suffering from fever produced by exposure to the sun and that this ointment is to cool her burning frame?'

recommended in ayurveda as a cure for heatstroke or fever. Interestingly, ayurveda also suggested the fragrance of vetiver to help ward off senility.[66]

As the number of aromatics available in ancient India grew, so too did the complexity of perfumes. Where at first perfumes offered to the gods—which was, of course, their original function—were limited to fresh, thornless flowers and incense of aloeswood and guggul, later texts from the eleventh and twelfth centuries mention several more materials,[67] including vetiver, that were being widely used. Offerings to deities were generally kept contemporary in this way.

Much later, the Mughals in their inimitable style began to use vetiver in the ways that still stand today—mats or tatties woven from the roots used as blinds that, when kept damp, could transform even a meagre dry breeze that blew through them to one that was fragrant and blessedly cool. The Imtiaz Mahal, the perfectly proportioned and symmetrical palace of the emperor at the Red Fort, had khus khanas at either end that were meant for summer repose, and would have been screened by these blinds. The mahal also had a teh khana or basement. This, of course, isn't accessible any longer, but as was pointed out during a guided historical walk of the fort, the large iron rings set above the arches that were used to hang draperies that changed along with the seasons: heavy quilted ones in the winter, vetiver blinds for the summer. A short

---

66. Naveen Patnaik, *The Garden of Life: An Introduction to The Healing Plants of India*, Aquarian/Harper Collins, Delhi, 1993, p. 171.

67. James McHugh, *Sandalwood and Carrion: Smell in Indian Religion and Culture*, Oxford University Press, New York, p. 239.

walk away from the fort, in a crowded lane and across from a large McDonald's outlet, there is an incongruously large haveli, a glimpse into another time. Haveli Khajanchi, as it is known, is said to have belonged to the royal treasurer, and though it is little more than a ruin now, it retains more than a touch of hauteur and architectural beauty with its delicate arches and grand use of marble. One needs only a bit of imagination to picture it as it would have been, its generous verandas shaded with fragrant khus blinds.

Similarly, sharbat, a Persian invention, made its way to India with the Mughals. The result was khus sharbat made from an extract of vetiver roots, bright green in colour (though this can likely be attributed to added food dye). It tastes like sweet, earthy, grass-green relief on a hot dusty day. Vetiver roots were often layered between woollen blankets and clothes as a moth repellent, but also perhaps to be reminded, in the depths of winter, that warmer days would return. And just as vetiver mats were a de facto cooling device in the air-conditionerless homes of the 1970s and 1980s, so were they used, quite ingeniously, by drivers to keep their cars from reaching baking temperatures in the summer sun. Khus mats were tied to the car's roof, and then wet every so often: an image that appears in perfect sepia tones in my mind.

In South India, vetiver is cultivated in vast plantations as well as smaller ones to provide farmers a little extra income. It is steam-distilled in huge boilers, and the essential oil makes its way into fine fragrances worldwide, including a few famous ones like Guerlain's *Vetiver*. The red-gold oil smells earthy, with notes of warm, sweet hay. It has a fine, elegant scent that lingers on the skin for long hours, becoming warmer and mellower as it settles in. Interestingly, it is always referred to very correctly as vetiver oil, distinguishable from the well-loved and familiar khus that grows unmonitored in the plains of North India. But it was this latter vetiver that I was curious to see harvested and distilled, and also eager to smell.

It is a fragrance that could be traced back for centuries that also holds a spot in my own memory. Back I went to UP. Not to Kannauj, the town that remains central to all conversation about traditional fragrance, but this time to Hasayan, a small town within the larger district of Hathras, where a lot of what Kannauj is famous for distilling grows. The seasons here are marked by harvests: roses, both damascena and centifolia varieties in the warmer weather, and khus in the winter. What makes the latter a bit more special is that it is one of the only remaining 'wild harvests'—technically not a harvest at all, as it is gathered from where it is found, collected and sold to be distilled. Trying to find out where exactly it grows, however, led me only to dead ends. Though I knew the facts, that it is a hardy grass, unremarkable in appearance, growing easily alongside roads, ponds, fields and railway tracks, and dug up by villagers during winter, it was still a 'harvest' I wanted to witness. I imagined myself in a remote area on a near-freezing morning alongside women with machetes hacking at the cold ground to get to the precious roots underneath. However, every inquiry I made about exact locations was met with resistance. Some said it wasn't safe, that khus was harvested in dark forests and distant swamps (which I took to mean that they did not know where it came from and didn't much care to), others that they knew but didn't want to tell me and have word get out since sources were increasingly limited, and some simply admitted to not knowing at all. Their business was the distillation. The material came to them through middlemen, and that was all they knew. And so, I made my peace with using my imagination to fill in that particular blank, and went on my way to Hasayan, and the succinctly named Hasayan Perfumers, where I had been invited to see the distillation.

I left on a January morning in the still dark with the sky a twilit blue and the expressway deserted but for a few motorcyclists returning from late shifts, bundled tight against the cold wind. The Yamuna, when I crossed it, was barely visible, the mist over it swirling like dry ice. It had been a while since I had made a road trip to this neighbouring state, and I was struck again by how one of the salient characteristics of the journey was relentless and incomplete construction work, evidenced by the eternal piles of debris by the roadside. While still in what constituted the National Capital Region (NCR), it seemed to serve a purpose—bridges, underpasses, massive buildings and such like—but further into UP, the unclaimed bricks and cement seemed as if they had permanently settled into the landscape. Where the smooth, modern, built-for-speed expressway ended, there was again that jagged seam where an entirely new area took over—one of verdant fields, brick huts, buffalo cart traffic and railway tracks, along the sides of which all of life plays out. Some of the villages I crossed were still shrouded in fog, the sun not having burnt it off yet. Looking toward the fields, I understood better why some of the distillers I had spoken to had tried to warn me away from wanting to see the harvest in action: the landscape was practically opaque.

Either by sheer luck or the power of my fervent wish to see khus growing in its natural habitat, we made a happy misturn. Thanks to an erroneously read map and a wrong turn, the last few kilometres of my journey were made on a narrow dirt track that ran between fields of mustard, wheat and potato, interrupted now and again by a canal with stagnant, slightly scummy water, but which had a wealth of weeds and grasses growing around it—much of it narrow, dense clumps of vetiver. Further along, their bright jackets visible in the fog that still hung over the area, young boys were squatting, digging around the roots to get what they could. So, not a swamp or dangerous forest after all, just a commonplace irrigation canal. This ability that North Indian vetiver possesses, to require nothing more than time and the predictability of seasons to regenerate itself every year, is what makes it unique. And it isn't only perfumers who value this wild grass. The *Vetiveria zizanoides* is primarily a cheap and natural solution to the problem of soil erosion when planted as a hedge. Its roots grow vertically for up to three metres and

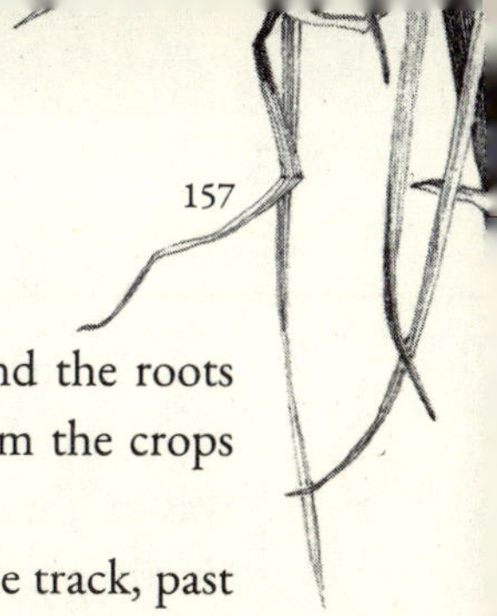

bind the soil, working as a 'botanical dam',[68] and the roots contain an oil that serves to keep rats at bay from the crops that are planted around it.

Another few kilometres of bumping along the track, past tiny villages, placid buffaloes and round-eyed children got me to the nagar panchayat of Hasayan. The sudden flurry of activity, concrete buildings and sounds came as a mild shock after the lull of the quiet fields. Past a busy market and through narrow paved lanes, I came to the other side of the town which had more open space, a few houses and a large iron gate behind which were the premises of the Hasayan Perfumers. Here again was a simple hydrodistillation unit. The 1.5-acre area was dominated by rows of copper degs set over earthen stoves, the roughly constructed tank of water in which the bhapkas, connected to the degs by twine-covered bamboo chongas, lay collecting the precious oil. Half-a-dozen men silently, efficiently worked at their tasks. It was neither the kind of work nor time of day that required loud voices. Everything was painted in shades of grey and dun. The raw concrete and brick structures, the dirt floor, bundles of firewood, the grey water and, billowing over it, giving it a slightly otherworldly air, the clouds of white steam rising from the tank and the smoke drifting off the stoves. A few pariah dogs lay draped over each other, close to the warmth of the banked stoves. In a corner, a young buffalo, tied to a

---

68. National Research Council, 1993, *Vetiver Grass: A Thin Green Line Against Erosion*, The National Academies Press, Washington, DC, https://doi.org/10.17226/2077.

stake in the ground, lowed mournfully at intervals. Above all of it, there was a sullen winter sky. Strange to think that it was on these cold mornings, leached of colour, that khus oil, the deep green essence of summer, was produced.

Rohit Jadaun, the young owner of Hasayan Perfumes and the third generation of his family to make a living by distilling the local grass that UP has always been known for, walked me through the simple set-up, stopping first at the small hillocks of vetiver (about 4,500 kilograms of the root in all) waiting their turn at the deg. He showed me how two lots, though they looked identical to me, were different. The first was distinguishable by its bundles of tiny root hairs clinging to bits of soil, chopped small. Called 'lachha' in the local trade lexicon, by the villagers doing the harvesting to the distillers, Jadaun said they had a higher oil yield than those in the adjoining pile, referred to as 'munjad', which had larger roots. However, although the latter produced less oil, he preferred it on account of the quality of the munjad oil.

This year, Jadaun is aiming to produce between 50–60 kilograms of oil. Distillation began in November and will carry on, rain or hail, till the end of February or for as long as the cold holds, since temperatures and oil yields are seemingly inversely proportional for this variety of khus.

Once the process begins, it takes on a life and rhythm of its own. After having been soaked for twenty-four hours to remove any earth still clinging to them, the roots are ready for the degs. There are a dozen degs here, each one able to hold 150 kilograms, with the distillation taking over two days. There are two workers for every four degs, and their work is intensive and skilled in ways that cannot be taught, only acquired. The degs must be filled with the right proportion of roots and water, tamped down and sealed deftly with a coil of clay mixed with coir fibres that are purpose-made. Firewood in the stove needs to be replenished now and again, but it's the job of the worker in charge to know just how much is needed to reach a required temperature. Once steam condenses in the bhapka, it is also for him to know, by touch, when it is full and needs to be replaced with a fresh one, and this has to be done seven times, perfectly every time, over two days with the deg 'resting' at night. If, in a particular year, the demand is especially high, that rest is sacrificed, and work carries on in shifts through the night. What is amply clear even in casual observation is just how labourious the work is, and how perfectly choreographed. As Jadaun points out to me: 'These men are kaarigars, not just labourers. The skills they have, have been passed down over generations and what we do here is not possible without them.'

While elsewhere industrialisation and modern technique have crept up on and transformed perfumery, it is remarkable how much the industry here still depends on human experience and craft. The only tools the kaarigars make use of are wooden mallets, cotton rags soaked in water and a sort of mop made of thick cotton-braided yarn on a stick, used to wipe out the inside of a bhapka after the oil has been poured out in order to get every last bit of oil that may be clinging to the rounded insides.

The insistence on sticking to these traditions isn't from lack of access to alternatives or a simple force of habit, but an absolute belief in the superiority of this time-tested method. Practically everywhere else in the world, vetiver is distilled by steam.

Some things are changing though. There are farmers in the north who have begun cultivating khus, as has been the norm in South India for decades. Like in the south, these new cultivations also use a hybrid, seedless variety of the grass that is high-yielding and better suited to steam distillation, most often done in massive industrial-sized boilers that can accommodate up to 3,000 kilograms of raw material, making them more efficient. But change comes slowly to an time-honoured craft so set in its ways. Jadaun remained convinced that the North Indian wild-harvested and hydrodistilled khus oil is unparalleled. 'That other oil feels different. The notes are very different, even the colour is completely different,' said Jadaun. To illustrate his point, he produced from a steel almirah a small glass bottle of emerald ruh khus for me to smell. I recognise it instantly as that same grassy, sweet smell with a hint of cool, wet soil that I have always found so moving.

In the end, it is, as most things are, a matter of simple preference and habit. There is no arguing with the fact that this wild variety is not high-yielding, giving up just about 35–50 grams of oil for 100 kilograms of grass.

Of course, the other essential factor to consider is the fact that the khus he processes grows at will within the limited radius of the larger Aligarh district with its particular soil and microclimatic conditions that directly affect the notes, giving it that secret, immortal something, which is yet to be recreated. It was also a revelation to me that the beautiful bottle-green colour is the result of the oil interacting with the uncoated copper that the deg is made of.

'Hathras district was created lately, but this khus is still known as Aligarh khus,' he informed me. He prides himself on being part of a larger unbroken tradition, harvesting and distilling the grass from the same places and in the same ways that his father and grandfather did, producing an oil that has come to be recognised for its quality.

Like any wild harvest though, this one also begs the inescapable question of unpredictability. Throughout our interaction, he lamented at various points the fact of low yields. Climate change has now made any forecasting even more uncertain. I asked him if he has any sort of plan or solution in mind for the future, but he seemed resigned to fate.

'There is not much we can do. Earlier there was less development, fewer fields and more wild areas to harvest from, but those have shrunk too, making it expensive now. Compared to how it was in my father's time, yields are very low, but if weather is good, it will be better. This is how it has always been.'

Currently, ruh khus runs between Rs 65,000–70,000 a kilogram, and the sheer rarity and unpredictability of it does certainly contribute to that figure. However, the prohibitively high cost of North Indian khus means that, like so many other beautiful ingredients produced in the country, it also tends to get adulterated, sometimes by adding oil from cultivated vetiver to it or, for the less nuanced, by adding odourless dioctyl phthalate for volume.

As with most ruhs and itrs produced in the country, the primary buyer for khus are the flavoured-tobacco and supari makers. They are reliable clients, can afford the prices and are just as cautious about adopting a change—being loath to mess with a good thing, in this case, a winning formula for a paan masala or supari that sells well.

The sun was getting higher, the interview was coming to a close. It was time to get back on the highway and head back to Delhi. On the way, I thought about how everything I had seen was an echo of how things were done a century or more ago, down even to adulteration. After all, traditional perfume has only ever reflected our collective human traits: an inescapable, quotidian greed and, equally, a love for nature and a longing for beauty to reflect on—it has always been, quite simply, one of our many mirrors.

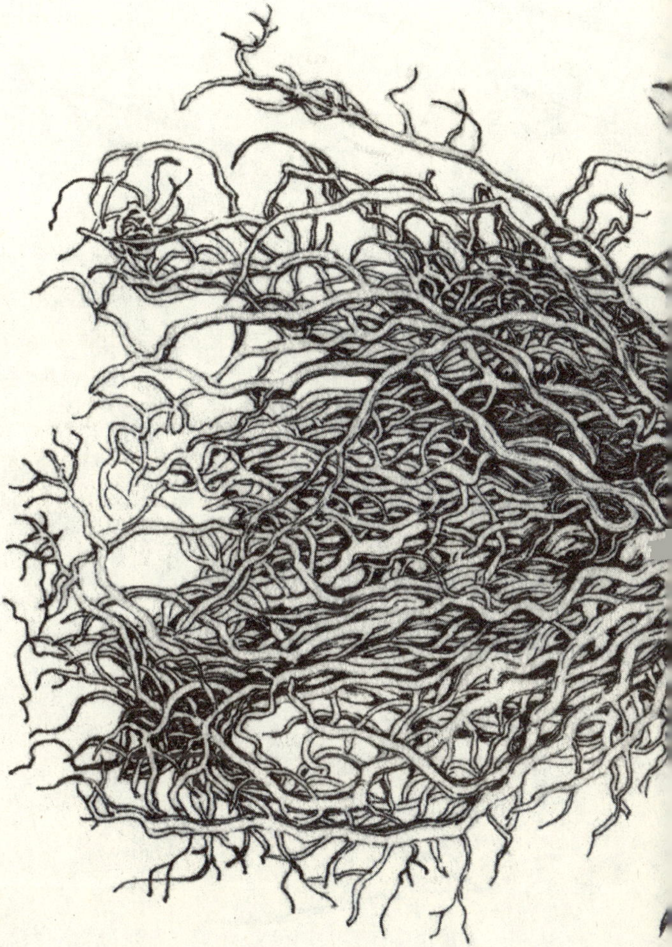

Postscript

AT THE END of my travels to states in all parts of the country I was asked by a friend what conclusions I'd arrived at regarding traditional perfumery and all I'd learnt of it. It was an obvious question, and an expected one. I gave it some thought. The truth is that it had been a process of discovery. I had learnt a lot, been surprised by much, even startled occasionally, and had shed quite a few ideas and notions that had been revealed to me as wrong.

In every state, with every grower and producer I had spoken to, I found more similarities than differences: a respect for the land and a dedication to the tradition, despite a growing frustration with factors beyond their control. Livelihoods dependant on the business of making itr and ruh have grown more fragile and the spectre of 'modern' perfumes isn't some imaginary hobgoblin.

Adaptation is essential. Between the glorious heyday of traditional fragrances and the vastly changed landscape of the present, the Indian perfume industry is hovering in a liminal space, one foot on either side, from where it could (and should) move forward.

And yet, I found in some places a quiet resistance. A recognition of the old methods and ingredients as valuable exactly for what they are. A belief that they could perhaps be brought into the modern fold.

Despite being buffeted by change wrought by climate, mechanisation and even the ephemeral nature of human fashions, the fact remains that traditional perfume works closely with the rhythms of the land, and touches many lives in the process of coming to be, as it has done for centuries. It is a craft composed of earth, water, fire, air and inspiration, and deserving of its place in the life and imagination of the country.

Acknowledgements

I AM INDEBTED TO the people who so generously offered me guidance, encouragement and information that I needed to be able to complete this book.

My deep thanks to the director and staff at FFDC Kannauj, Mr Jain at Pragati Aroma, Mr Palaniswamy at Jasmine CE, Dr Ramakantha at the Wood Sciences Institute, Bangalore, Rakib Ahmad at Bharat Saffron, Zakir Hussain Laskar, Mr Bikash Baruah, Rohit Jadaun in Hasayan and Pranjal Kapoor at M.L. Ram Narain perfumers.

My thanks also to my agent, Kanishka Gupta, and my editor and publisher at Westland for taking a chance on this book. To Saurabh Garge, Nirupa Rao, Jignesh Jhaveri and Prashish More, for their brilliant ability to add a visual element to my words. To Shruti Debi, for all her help and encouragement way back when this book was half-formed.

To my family and friends, I am forever grateful for your support, patience and faith in me.